Rivers, Rogues, and Timbermen

in the Novels of Brainard Cheney

Rivers, Rogues, and Timbermen

in the Novels of Brainard Cheney

by

Michael R. Williams, Jr.

MM John Welda BookHouse

2015

Published in 2015 by MM John Welda BookHouse
P.O. Box 111, Eastman, Georgia 31023

For more information on this book and the author:
http://www.lightwood.com

The Lightwood History Collection: Book 7

ISBN: 978-0-9907009-5-1 (Hardcover)

Portions of this work originally appeared in 2003 as a master's thesis for degree candidacy at Valdosta State University, Georgia, under the title: *Rivers, Rogues, and Timber Wars: Agrarianism in the Novels of Brainard Cheney*

Front Cover: Detail from an 1890 map of Georgia

CONTENTS

Brainard Cheney, 1941 researching *River Rogue* on the Ocmulgee River

To the Reader

Why Brainard Cheney?

Georgia author Brainard Cheney published four novels in his lifetime: *Lightwood* (1939), *River Rogue* (1942), *This is Adam* (1958), and *Devil's Elbow* (1969). Of these, only the first received much critical attention, and none sold many copies. They all went out of print soon after publication, although *Lightwood* and *River Rogue* were reprinted in paperback form during the 1980s to celebrate the Restoring Altamaha Folk Traditions (R.A.F.T.) festival. However, in 2012, MM John Welda BookHouse began releasing Cheney's novels once again, this time in glorious hardcover and ebook, as well as trade paperbacks. The republication of the Brainard Cheney novels has led to a revival of interest in Cheney. His relevance has never been greater. I hope that a new generation of Georgians will embrace these books by their native son.

Cheney deserves more notice than he received for several reasons. His gift for description is remarkable and compares with some of the better naturalist writers of the 19th century. He is one of the finest writers to portray the 19th and early 20th century Georgia Wiregrass region, particularly the

Altamaha River area and its floodplain. Anyone interested in the area and its history cannot afford to ignore Cheney's work. Few have ever written about the region Cheney describes. None have done so as skillfully as he has, particularly in his first three novels.

Secondly, these novels are important for their historical nature alone. Cheney's fictional accounts of the Georgia Squatters War offer a far better picture than any of the historical accounts, at least until the publication of *The Dodge Land Wars* (2004) and *The Lightwood Chronicles* (2012) within the last ten years. It is likely these historians chose to document the real events only after reading Cheney's fictionalized version in *Lightwood* and to a lesser extent *River Rogue*. Violence consumed the Wiregrass region after the Civil War. These events were both tragic and preventable. They are definitely worthy of study, as Cheney's work captures the spirit of the Squatters War better than any other document I have read on the matter.

But even were it not for these events, Cheney's novels would still be of historical interest for anyone concerned with the habits, customs, and manner of speaking of squatters, settlers, farmers, timber men, rafters, and steamboat captains in the 19th century in Wiregrass Georgia. I first encountered these novels as an adolescent at the home of my grandparents, Barclay and Woody Williams. Later, at the University of Georgia, I took a Southern dialect class that required me to analyze the use of dialect in a work of fiction. I chose *River*

Rogue by Cheney. I went into it with no preconception of whether the dialect was accurate or not. I had always found some of the speech patterns in his novels bizarre, particularly the lack of the postvocalic "r" in the rafts-men's speech in *River Rogue*. (For example, Cheney's river men say "ovah theah" for "over there" and so forth.) In the course of my research, I found all of Cheney's dialect confirmed. He conducted meticulous research for that novel, and the stories and turns of phrase all came from authentic former rafts-men. His work with dialect rivals that of Mark Twain's *The Adventures of Huckleberry Finn*.

While attending Vanderbilt, Cheney was associated with a literary group of conservative Southern writers known as the Agrarians. The Agrarians opposed mechanization of agriculture, industrialization, and integration of schools. For these reasons, I have often heard it said that the Agrarians have been debunked. Even members of the group, such as Robert Penn Warren, later admitted that they were mistaken on many of these issues, most notably segregation.

There are elements, however, of agrarianism, such as the emphasis on conservation of resources, which are still relevant today. In addition, Cheney stood out from the Agrarians. He was younger and in many ways, more progressive than the other members of the group. He embraced the social programs of the New South in a way that they did not. Partly raised by a black man himself, he was more progressive on racial issues as well. His letters to Flannery O'Connor reveal a man who approved and applauded *Brown vs. Board of Education* and who condemned demagoguery and corrupt politicians at every turn. Cheney worked in politics for many years. His nephew Roy Neel served as Vice President Al Gore's Chief of Staff. Cheney's political views and his concern over the fate of the Georgia rivers that he loved have proven prescient. They have been confirmed by time and history.

For a southerner, Brainard Cheney was a man ahead of his time. He was less well known than some of his contemporaries and colleagues, such as Robert Penn Warren, John Crowe Ransom, or Flannery O'Connor. Yet his novels display moments of brilliance and even greatness.

Preface

The subject of this text is a little-known Georgia author named Brainard Cheney. While attending Vanderbilt University in the mid 1920s, Cheney became affiliated with the Agrarian/Fugitive group. He spent most of his life deeply engaged in Tennessee politics. He published four novels in his lifetime, some of which were well-reviewed, none of which gained any real prominence. Still, the historical and literary importance of these novels continues to grow. Their deepest value lies in their ability to capture the spirit of life in this historically neglected region. His four published novels, *Lightwood* (1939), *River Rogue* (1942), *This is Adam* (1958), and *Devil's Elbow* (1969), all chronicle certain aspects of life and historical events in the Wiregrass region of South Georgia.

Cheney came from a prominent family in the Wiregrass Region. His father was a lawyer, who had at one time been involved in the litigation between the Georgia Land and Lumber Company and the settlers of Telfair and Dodge counties. This event later became known as the Georgia Squatters War and would inspire Cheney's first novel, *Lightwood*. The purpose of this book is to analyze Cheney's novels historically and literarily and to offer some commentary on the historical events that inspired them.

Cheney's father was from Telfair County but briefly moved across the river in the late 19th century to the town of Fitzgerald, Georgia. Cheney was born there on June 3, 1900, to Mattie Mood Cheney and Colonel Brainard B. Cheney.

Just two years later, right across the Ocmulgee river, on Christmas Eve night in Telfair County, Georgia, near the town of Jacksonville, a Christmas tree-lighting celebration had just ended at a rural church, built on the site of an old Indian fort near the Ocmulgee River. One of the churchgoers stepped outside, carrying his infant daughter in his arms. Adjusting his coat against the winter wind, he felt in his pockets for his pipe and set the little girl down for a moment. As he lit his pipe, shots rang out and he fell dead, bleeding out into the cold Georgia dust. Children and adults alike screamed and scattered.

A few miles down the road, a local farmer riding home in a wagon with his wife and infant child heard the shots, shivered, and spurred his horses homeward. No one was ever charged with the crime. The local community helped protect the identity of the murderer. The grand jury concluded that the man had been killed by "persons unknown." The homicide was considered justifiable in light of the turmoil the victim and his compatriots had wrought on the region. This was the final shot fired in what later became known as the Georgia Squatters War.

You cannot address the Squatters War without mentioning the geography of the Wiregrass region of Georgia, and you cannot discuss this region without grappling with the three great rivers of South Georgia that form the Altamaha River system. It is challenging to state exactly where the Altamaha River system begins. This great south Georgia river is formed from two rivers that begin in north Georgia, the Ocmulgee and the Oconee.

You could make a decent argument that the Ocmulgee begins behind a Kroger store at the intersection of Hardee Street and Moreland Avenue near the Little Five Points region of Atlanta. Little Five Points was an old stomping ground of mine in college. I find a nice symmetry in the notion that during my sojourn in Atlanta, I was only a few feet away from the origins of the mighty river alongside whose banks I played as a child and in whose waters I first learned to swim. The stream that begins here as a ditch amid the industrial behemoth of Atlanta, Georgia, becomes known as Sugar Creek as it flows ever southward, eventually becoming the South River as it leaves Atlanta.

A similar argument could be made for Intrenchment Creek, which starts in Brownwood Park, also right off Moreland Avenue. It also flows into the South River, which meets the Yellow and Alcovy Rivers at Lake Jackson. Where the water from these streams flows over the dam at Lake Jackson, it is known as the Ocmulgee River. The Ocmulgee River flows south from Lake Jackson through the towns of Macon, Hawkinsville, and Abbeville, and then makes a great turn southeastward through what is known as the Big Bend section. From there it flows eastward through Jacksonville and Lumber City, Georgia, and then into the Oconee River, forming the Altamaha and from there to the coast where it meets the Atlantic Ocean at Darien.

This river system occupies a major role in Georgia's destiny. The Oconee was the original boundary line separating the white settlements from the Creek Nation. This was established by the Treaty of Fort Wilkinson in 1802. The Treaty of Washington three years later moved the boundary westward to the Ocmulgee River and opened the lands between the rivers to settlement by white men.

The men who moved into this territory were the first Georgian pioneers, and they faced the same hardships and challenges as their later compatriots did along the Western frontier. The exploits of these Western settlers have long been celebrated in print and movies while the Georgia settlers have been neglected by historians and fiction writers alike. Nevertheless, they too fought in skirmishes for their survival in these early years. They made their homes along the banks of these rivers. They settled along the Ocmulgee and travelled along the river itself or the River Road, which ran parallel with the river from Macon to Darien.

The vast forests of longleaf timber remained sparsely settled. This region is known alternately as the Pine Barrens region of Georgia or the Wiregrass region of Georgia, terms used interchangeably in the book that follows. The value of the pine trees at the time was enormous, but there was no infrastructure in place to ship them to the sawmill.

In the 1830s, a sawmill was established at the confluence of the Ocmulgee and Oconee Rivers along the Little Ocmulgee River in Telfair County, Georgia, near present day Lumber City. The sawmill ultimately failed due the difficulty in shipping timber down the variable river, where water levels were prone to fall drastically in summer to the point where they could not sustain barge traffic. Deeds to much of this land changed hands rapidly in the ensuing years, a large portion being sold at tax sales and redistributed to the pioneer settlers moving into the area. Following the end of the Civil War, northern industrialists acquired the original deed to the 300,000 acres of pine trees between the rivers. With the construction of the Macon and Brunswick Railroad, shipping the timber to the port city of Darien was established and now possible. The Dodge Company began harvesting the timber on a massive scale. In time, the Dodges took local landowners to court in "ejectment" suits, claiming the settlers illegally occupied company land. The resulting land disputes engulfed the region in violence and conflict for a period of at least 50 years until all the timber had been cut and the industrialists retreated to their northern enclaves or their graves.

Unspeakable violence reigned through the region at this time, culminating with a murder in a church courtyard on Christmas Eve night in full view of the congregation and the children who had just lighted the Christmas tree. Brainard Cheney, a Lumber City native, chose to subsequently document many of these events in his four Altamaha River novels.

This work explores the meaning of Cheney's novels and their historical basis through the lens of the Agrarian literary movement that originated at Vanderbilt University. Cheney's novels portray the early settlers of the region as living in a sort of agrarian idyll which is later disrupted by potent economic and social forces, first symbolized in Coventry and Company, the timber company that plays a villainous role in his first two novels. Racial strife and corruption, both economic and sexual, also play roles. His later novels reflect his personal conversion to Catholicism and feature characters who gain redemption only by turning to God. The tragedy of Cheney's novels always occurs when the characters abandon their simple existence based on land and river cycles for the lure of secular urban life and the corruption that comes with it. And just like in history, the settlers fall helpless before the overwhelming power of unfettered capitalism, which reigns supreme over the land.

1.

Brainard Cheney, Lucius Williams, and the Georgia Squatters War

One of the Ruskin boys had better luck a Sunday night later that fall. Deacon and his wife and baby had come out of Blockhouse Church after the evening meeting and were standing on the steps. There were church-goers ahead of them leaving, but no one in sight to be suspicious of. Deacon had filled his pipe in church and he handed his wife the baby so he could light it. He struck the match but never got it lit.

—Brainard Cheney, from his novel *Lightwood*

The Georgia Squatters War took place within the Wiregrass Region of Georgia in the middle portion of the state between the Ocmulgee and Oconee Rivers, primarily around the region of the Ocmulgee known as the Big Bend, which today comprises Dodge and Telfair counties. This historical event has received little attention outside of the region in which it occurred, and indeed, most modern residents of Telfair and Dodge County know little to nothing about the conflict. Time and ecological change have obscured these events and their causes. In fact, most of the people living within the Wiregrass region of Georgia in the 21st century have never seen a blade of wiregrass and have little notion of what their own environment must have looked like in the late 19th century.

The term "wiregrass" does not simply denote a form of grass. It denotes an entire ecosystem, one that is unique to the Pine Barrens region of Georgia, and one that is in great peril. Imagine what our region looked like one hundred and fifty years ago. It was composed of vast forests of 100-foot-tall longleaf pines with tufts of wiregrass as the sole undergrowth. Our ancestors hunted, worked, and farmed in these forests, and that is where our region got its name.

This ecosystem was so vast that it was assumed to be permanent. Unfortunately, after the Civil War, northern industrialists moved into the region (specifically, William E. Dodge and William Pitt Eastman, from Maine, after whom Dodge County and Eastman, Georgia are named). Under disputed title they claimed much of the land between the Ocmulgee and Oconee Rivers, expelled many families from their homes, and harvested much of the virgin pine timber. Outside of the families involved in the conflict, few remember the details of this historical event that took place over a period of decades after the Civil War. The families who lost land in the Squatters War have long been forgotten along with the ecological and personal destruction wrought by these events.

The legal cases involved are complex and difficult to follow. Brainard Cheney's first novel skillfully portrays this conflict and the loss of this incredible stand of virgin timber, along with the lives of many of the local settlers. His later novels also take place in the region and document the negative effects of a corrupt capitalist system that threatens the way of life of the people living in the Wiregrass region. His novels are important both as literature and history, and seek to preserve a forgotten heritage. Those of us living in the region would do well to read them and embrace our history and heritage.

I first became interested in Cheney's novels and Wiregrass history as a child. My grandparents, Barclay and Woody Williams, had copies of the novels *Lightwood* and *River Rogue* in their homes, as well as *The Land Pirates* by Marion Erwin and Addie Garrison Briggs' *They Don't Make People Like They Used To*. My family played a role in the Georgia Squatters War. Like my distant cousin Roy Cowart, who details his connection to these events in *The Dodge Land Troubles* and *The Lightwood Chronicles*, I descend from some of the earliest European settlers of Telfair County, Georgia. Jane Walker and Chris Trowell's *The Dodge Land Troubles* along with Stephen Whigham's *The Lightwood Chronicles* are the best historical records of these events, and I cannot improve upon them. I would, however, like to discuss the relationship between my family's history in Telfair County and Brainard Cheney's first novel, *Lightwood*.

Joseph Williams, Jr. (1760-1851)

The patriarch of our family in Telfair was Lt. Joseph Williams, Jr., a Revolutionary War veteran. His grave marker is in the Blockhouse Cemetery, near Jacksonville, Georgia. What little I know about Joseph is that his farm was apparently located in China Hill, Georgia, near where my family still lives today, probably at or near some of the land currently owned by the Boone family. He came from Duplin County, North Carolina. He was born there on December 20, 1760. He entered in the service of the Revolutionary army as a volunteer in 1779 and was promoted to first lieutenant, commanded by Captain Aaron Williams, possibly his brother. Much later in his life, a local politician revoked his pension on the grounds of insufficient evidence that he had fought in the war. Addie Briggs states that this was due to anger over a race for Telfair County Clerk of Superior Court. His pension was later reinstated with the help of several local citizens who testified to his service in the Revolutionary War. He claims in his pension documents that he was in no general engagement but was involved in skirmishes with the British and Tories, the main one being about ten miles north of Wilmington, North Carolina.

Joseph moved to Telfair County in 1823 and apparently died on April 10, 1851, which would put him at the age of 90. An obituary I located lists his age at the time at a remarkable 104 years, but this is obviously incorrect and contradicts his own sworn testimony as to his age in his efforts to reclaim his pension.

Joseph's daughter Elizabeth married her first cousin John, the son of Joseph's brother, Byrd. Their children were Emily, Lucius, and Joseph Gooden Williams. Joseph Gooden was my great-great-great grandfather. His son Ben at some point moved across the river into Irwin County but came back across the river in 1895 and purchased the family farm in China Hill where I still live today.

Captain Lucius L. Williams was my great-great-great-great uncle. Both of these men played a prominent role in the land struggles. Historian Addie Briggs has written extensively about Lucius's role, as have Jane Walker, Chris Trowell, and Roy Cowart. However, I believe that I can add to what has been written about the history and shed some light on the historical nature of Brainard Cheney's first novel, *Lightwood*.

Lucius Lazarus Williams (1834-1895)

Much has already been written about Lucius Williams. It is hard to separate the man from the myth at this point, but I believe I can construct a creditable narrative from all the various sources. Brainard Cheney includes the Lucius Williams story in *Lightwood*, basing the character of Jock Ruskin on his life and death. In history, Lucius's death occurred after the murder of Captain John Forsyth and the main action in Cheney's novel. In *Lightwood*, Cheney presents these events as occurring before Forsyth's death in order to escalate the dramatic tension in this work of historical fiction.

The conflict between the Dodge Company and the locals is often referred to as the Squatters War. This work will use that term exclusively to refer to the conflict. There were two major court cases on which the Squatters War hinged. The first case involved the murder of John C. Forsyth. The second was a series of huge land ejectment cases such as *Norman W. Dodge vs. Lucius Williams, et al.*, which bundled all of the Dodge land claims into one suit. Cheney's novel focuses primarily on the murder of John Forsyth, but the final tragedy of the novel is sealed by the second case. The character Micajah Corn returns home from testifying against his family and friends in the murder case only to find that the company has taken his lands along with those of his neighbors and compatriots.

In 1894, the Supreme Court of Georgia overruled its previous decision for the Dodge Company, but the company soon after filed a bill of peace in the federal court that named 381 defendants, including Lucius Williams. He was a man of great tenacity and determination. Trowell and Walker contend that Dodge may have "met his match" in the person of Lucius Williams. Addie Briggs calls him "an outstanding man in the community [...] always ready to help a neighbor."[1]

A historian told me ten years ago that I should be proud to have Lucius as my ancestor—that he was a hero of the lost cause of the Squatters War. I had never thought of him as a hero, at least not in any traditional sense. He was evidently a brutal man, capable of rage and acts of violence in certain situations, but he seems also to have been a kind man, deeply respected in the region. A photo of him and his second wife reveals a stern figure in a black frock coat and hat with long white beard attached to a surprisingly youthful face. At any rate, he was a formidable opponent to the Dodges, and he embarrassed them and the federal agents on several occasions. The story of his life and death comprises one of the great stories of Telfair County and the Dodge Land Wars. While a somewhat peripheral character in Cheney's novel, he emerges as the central figure in the historical record of these events.

Lucius was born in 1833 and served several terms as sheriff of Telfair County. During the Civil War, he enlisted in the

Georgia Volunteer Infantry and served in the Army of Northern Virginia under Company B, 49th regiment, the Telfair Volunteers. He was elected 2nd lieutenant March 4, 1862, 1st lieutenant December 29, 1862, and finally Captain February 23, 1864. He was captured at Petersburg, Virginia, on April 2, 1865.[2]

Lucius's regiment saw major action at almost all of the major battles in the eastern theater of the war. The National Park Service characterizes the losses of his regiment in the following manner:

> The 49th took an active part in the campaigns of the army from Seven Pines to Cold Harbor, fought in the Petersburg trenches south of the James River, and was involved in the Appomattox operations. It reported 68 casualties at Second Manassas and 61 at Fredericksburg. The unit lost thirteen percent of the 280 at Chancellorsville and more than twenty-five percent of the 329 at Gettysburg. It surrendered with 8 officers and 103 men.[3]

Lucius must have witnessed countless horrors and unspeakable violence in these battles. Several historians have noted that Lucius was captured at Petersburg and spent some time in a Federal prison camp. I think it worthwhile to revisit the terrible Siege of Petersburg, which does not receive enough attention historically. It was the longest campaign of the war, nearly a year of brutal trench warfare, foreshadowing the terrible fighting and conditions that would later come to prominence in World War I.

During the early months of 1865, Grant had cut off all the roads into Petersburg. Sherman was advancing rapidly on Lee's rear, who was faced with the inevitability of being surrounded if he did not retreat.

James McPherson notes that on April 1, 1865, Sheridan's cavalry finally defeated Pickett's two divisions of infantry. Pickett's "divisions collapsed half of their men surrendering to the whooping Yankees and the other half running rearward in rout."[4] According to McPherson: "When the news reached Grant that evening, he ordered an assault all along the line next morning."[5] The next morning would have been April 2, the date of Lucius's capture: "At dawn it came, with more élan and power than the Army of the Potomac had shown for a long time."[6] The rebels fought desperately as they fell back, but it was only to hold on to the inner defenses until dark in order to escape. The Union army punched through Confederate lines at several places southwest of the city. In the ensuing chaos, many men were captured and killed. Lucius Williams was one of those captured.

It is significant that Lucius was captured during a retreat, and it probably explains his refusal to retreat or surrender thirty years later in his confrontation with the Dodge Company and the agents of the federal court. After his capture, Lucius was initially sent to Old Capitol Prison at Washington, DC. Later he was transferred to Johnson's Island, Ohio, and eventually released on June 24, 1865[7]. He must have been painfully aware that if he had held on a few more days, the war would have been over. He could have surrendered with Lee at Appomattox and been sent home. Instead he spent nearly three months in a federal prison camp.

I have read posts on message boards online claiming that Lucius was captured and escaped five times during the Civil War and other obvious exaggerations. One finds no evidence of this in the historical record, but it is a testament to the myth that surrounds the man that people could believe this about him. He has been endowed with legendary status by his descendants.

Lucius Williams enters the Dodge story on a spectacular scale in December of 1894. He was obviously already on the Dodge's radar. He lived in Telfair County near Cobbville on the China Hill Road, which connects modern day Highway 441 with Highway 117. His lands were among those claimed by Dodge.

It seems clear that Lucius had been engaged in small actions of interference against the Dodges for years beforehand. Family lore and Addie Briggs both point to the fact that Lucius was skilled at forging the kinds of "coffee pot" deeds that

Calhoun Calebb talks about in the novel *Lightwood*. In the novel and in history, local families residing on the land under adverse possession without clear title would often forge deeds to the land to help validate their claims in court. Forgers often soaked the phony deeds in coffee to give them an aged appearance. My father has always suggested that Lucius was involved in other subtle acts of "terrorism" against the company forcibly evicting his neighbors from their lands. Lucius may have helped sabotage the tram roads built on or near his lands, or he may have driven spikes into logs to damage the company mills. Briggs points out his reputation for "sniping at the timber men."[8] In *Lightwood*, Cheney describes the fictional Lucius Williams, whom he calls Jock Ruskin, in the following manner:

> Jock was a fleshy, red-faced, Irish kind of fellow, who talked faster than common and was always ready to fight—and he had plenty of nerve, but was a little apt to bulldoze. His three boys—those that were his by blood—were pretty much like him. Jock and his boys had headed up most of the fight against the company from Coventry Boom to Jacksonville. They had led the band to burn tramroads, to loose the rails, to burn turpentine boxes, to drive spikes into sawlogs, and

they were always ready to give a hand in running log-choppers off of anybody's land.[9]

In Cheney's novel, the company agent, Zenas Fears, was
personally "out to get" Lucius. Historically, Lucius had more
trouble with the federal judge Emory Speer and marshal John
Kelly out of Macon than any particular agent of the company.
The final ejectment suit was named against "Lucius Williams,
et al.," so it seems clear that the Dodge Company already regarded him as their chief adversary in the county. Lucius, of
course, ignored his summons to appear at the federal court in
Macon.

On December 9, 1894, the court sent three deputy marshals to arrest Lucius and Stephen Williams for contempt of
court. The officers, John Kelley, J.C. Thomas, and W.L. Poore,
arrived in a buggy from Jacksonville, Georgia. Deciding that
the buggy was imprudent, they hid in waiting behind his
house and sent their buggy back to Jacksonville. Lucius must
have already been suspicious because the *Macon Telegraph*
reports that the officers from their vantage point watched an
armed Lucius and George Morris Williams following their
buggy tracks around his home. Lucius then sent George Williams to follow the tracks toward Jacksonville. A while later,
he went into his home and left his gun there.

According to the deputies, when he emerged from the
home, they notified Lucius of who they were and attempted to

arrest him. At this point he yelled out to his cousin George to "notify his friends that the rascals had taken him and to come at once, and that he would never be taken before the United States court alive."[10] Of course, Lucius had already been "taken alive" by agents of the federal government nearly 30 years before and had spent months rotting in a US prison camp. Like Micajah Corn in Cheney's *Lightwood*, Lucius probably did not differentiate between the Union Army and the Dodge Company in his mind. Both consisted of Yankees organized on a massive scale and hostile to his own interests. Micajah, at the beginning of *Lightwood,* imagines the company and its employees as a "uniformed antpile" and thinks: "So the Yankee army threatened him again."[11]

At any rate, if the account in the *Macon Telegraph* is to be believed, Lucius displayed incredible bravery and recklessness in the face of the threat from the federal officers now attempting to arrest him. He began to move at a rapid pace towards his rifle after the marshals announced their intentions. According to the report, "Deputy Marshall John Kelly then threw his gun to his shoulder and pointed it at Williams and commanded him to halt and surrender. Williams then said Kelly could shoot and be damned, that he [Lucius] had but a short time to live and he [Kelly] would not cut him out of many days and he would die before he would go before the United States Court, that he did not expect to be arrested alive."[12]

13

Lucius clearly used some coarse language in this conflict. Later accounts of his words at the time are censored out of newspaper reports. W.B. Fussell noted at trial that Williams "was wicked" and did not use "Sunday School language."[13]

Lucius represented a new kind of adversary for the Dodge Company, the most dangerous kind. Here they encountered a man who did not care whether he lived or died, a man who would rather be martyred in the cause than to submit in any way to their wishes. In fact, reading this account, one finds it remarkable that Lucius Williams lived as long as he did. In hindsight, it seems inevitable that he would die at the hands of the company agents or the federal marshals.

These initial charges do not seem serious enough to warrant Lucius's violent reaction, but clearly he would not allow himself to be arrested for any reason. He and Marshal Kelly wound up in a nail-biting struggle over the gun. Meanwhile, D. O. Kelly, Lucius's son-in-law, brought out his rifle from the house. Marshal Poore thoroughly covered him, telling Kelly that he would kill him, causing D. O. Kelly to lower his gun. Marshal John Kelly eventually got handcuffs on Lucius. Accounts of the later murder trial against Marshal Kelly suggest that Lucius tried to stab Kelly to death and nearly succeeded.[14]

If the officers' account is correct, the next segment reveals a lot about Lucius. According to them, he became enraged at his son-in-law and begged him to shoot the marshals, abusing him for being a coward. He said that "he never thought his son-in-law would stand by and see him handcuffed." This sort of language becomes a common theme with Lucius throughout these accounts. It is significant because had D. O. Kelly shot the marshals, he himself would almost certainly have been killed. Lucius stated earlier that he did not care for his own life because he had "but a short time to live." His actions here make it clear that he expected his son-in-law to be willing to die to defend Lucius as well, which is a different story. The son-in-law's decision to allow Lucius to be taken rather than have them all die right there in the yard seems reasonable to a modern reader, but it was not reasonable for Lucius. For Lucius, the code was everything. This was a war: one that you had to be willing to die fighting.

The story becomes more amusing at this point. The marshals agreed to let D. O. Kelly keep his gun if he would not point it at them, and they began the long march on foot to Jacksonville, Georgia. They were met upon the road by the wives of their prisoners who said that they would have the officers "mobbed."[15] Marshall Kelly then claimed to encounter a violent, armed mob of Williamses and friends, loudly threatening to kill him, Thomas, and Poore. Williams, echoing his earlier comments to his son-in-law, then "held up his hands to the crowd and said that he never thought he would live to see his relatives and countrymen allow him to be handcuffed by a set of rascals, and called upon them to shoot the

officers." Again, Lucius amazes in his ruthlessness and determination, and willingness to play on the guilt of his relatives
to see himself freed.

At this point a member of the mob again called D. O.
Kelly's courage into question, cursing him for not using his
gun on the marshals and said, "'If you don't use the gun, give
it to me and I will use it.'" The story goes that D. O. Kelly then
laid down his gun and allowed a member of the mob to pick it
up. At this point there was a general parley where the marshals agreed to allow Williams to give bond in Jacksonville
and not be carried to the Macon Court (apparently, the son-
in-law D. O. Kelly was justice of the peace and would have
been able to give the bond personally). George Morris Williams stated that he would gladly put up a $50,000 bond as
soon as they reached the destination. This never happened,
however, as the mob forced the marshals to return to Lucius's
house and retrieve the key to his handcuffs. After he had been
released, the marshals headed back to Macon, not bothering
to take their horses and buggy.

A major player in this event was Judge Emory Speer, who
presided over all of the Dodge cases in Federal Court and who
had directed the marshals to arrest Lucius. Judge Speer's account claims that Williams "violently" resisted the marshals
"with every exertion of force possible to him [...] refused to
receive the paper and assaulted one of the officers, and sent
out immediately running to his desperate associates in the

neighborhood to assemble and rescue him from the custody of the officers."[16] The language of Speer's account is ambiguous and his account therefore dubious. He was undoubtedly biased against Williams. His account is contradictory in nature. If Williams had "sent out running" to his compatriots, how then could he have been in need of rescue? Speer makes it sound as if Williams were never taken into custody in the first place.

A December 12, 1894, article in the *Macon Telegraph* stated that Lucius had been freed when the marshals by happenstance came across a group of Lucius's friends at a church meeting. By New Year's Eve, the story had changed. A letter to the editor of the *Macon Telegraph*, written anonymously by citizens of Telfair County and published on December 31 of that year states the following:

> The officers passed within a few hundred yards of a school house, where the people had gathered for Sunday School, which had just adjourned. The marshals in seeing the crowd of Sunday School people coming in their direction asked Williams what it meant, and he was sharp enough to turn the circumstances to his advantage by informing the officers that it was a crowd of his friends and that they had better 'burn the wind' in getting away from

there. They took Williams at his word and made a beeline for McRae, not even taking time to go a mile out of their way to get their teams.[17]

This account also seems doubtful, an intentional effort to ridicule the marshals for cowardice, written by Telfair authors sympathetic to Lucius. It is hard to discern which element is true. It seems possible that a Sunday School party or church meeting did play a role in Lucius's rescue since it was mentioned in two of these accounts, obviously related by different people weeks apart. Also, the events occurred on a Sunday morning. However, the marshals' account is probably true in the essential details. The marshals themselves do not always appear heroic in their own version. Their account of having to return to Lucius's house to retrieve the key lost in the scuffle strikes a reader as realism, an unnecessary detail to add if the narrative were false. This negates the notion that they fled in terror at the sight of a "Sunday School class," which connotes a group of harmless children. In fact, a later article in the *Telegraph* specifically stated that they were "Sunday School children."[18] Again it seems unlikely that the marshals, who clearly demonstrated some bravery in capturing the elusive and dangerous Lucius, would have run from children. Some of the men who made up the mob may have been involved in a Sunday School group (although even this seems unlikely), but regardless, they were no less terrifying when they arrived at the scene armed and threatening to shoot the officers.

The next event in the Lucius Williams saga occurred on January 20, 1895, when some unknown men shot into a crowd of Dodge timber cutters on Lucius's son's land and "dangerously wounded" one of them.[19] On January 28, a posse of marshals headed by Harrell arrested five men suspected of having rescued Lucius in the earlier affray. Among them were "W. B. Fussell and M. McCormick of Irwin county and Henry Fussell, Aleck Fussell, and Bob Williams of Telfair."[20] In addition, these marshals, no doubt embarrassed by their earlier humiliation at the hands of the mob, resorted to outright lawlessness and tyranny by arresting and holding hostage my great-great grandfather, Ben Williams.

Ben Williams (1850-1926)

Ben Williams was born in Telfair County probably around the China Hill area. For the most part, these River Road Williamses did not share in the plight of the "squatters" out in the county. The Dodge Company did not claim much land around the River Road. These lands were cypress swamps, filled with hardwood timber, not longleaf pines, and most of these settlers occupied the land since the 1820s.

In the novel *Lightwood,* the River Road people are distinguished from other settlers like the Corns when Micajah first travels to Lancaster (a fictionalized Eastman). In the novel, Cheney describes the crowd as "mixed," and he compares the "block-wheeled carts" like Micajah drove to the more elegant buggies with "fringe around their tops" with black coachmen "dressed in linen dusters" driven by the River Road families[21]. Also, the ladies from around the River Road, Hawkinsville, and Lumber City are dressed in "blue and pink and yellow and white and silver-colored dresses." The men wear "jimswinger coats and striped breeches."[22] This clothing stands in stark contrast with the other women who wear home-made hats made of shucks and palmetto. Their men wear "brown jeans britches and rawhide shoes and homespun shirts and jackets."[23]

Despite the fact that Ben Williams did not live on land claimed by Dodge, he was caught up in the turmoil of the times. Lucius Williams was his uncle, and the men were married to sisters at the time. Lucius's second wife was Margaret McDermid, and Ben's first wife was Mary McDermid. We can be certain that he was aware of his uncle's troubles with the Dodge Company, but why was he arrested? Was he among the men who rescued Lucius Williams in the earlier struggle? It seems unlikely. No one in my family has ever made such a claim.

At this point in time, Ben lived in Irwin County (now Ben Hill County) in the Dickson's Mill community, near present day Fitzgerald, Georgia. He operated the mill along with old man Dickson. Dickson's Old Mill Pond still exists a short distance off Highway 107 between Jacksonville, Georgia, and Fitzgerald, Georgia. The old mill pond is located near the intersection of modern day Sturgeon Creek Road and Dickson's Mill Pond Road.

This was a short distance across the Ocmulgee River on the China Hill (Boney's Ferry) ferry from Ben's family's old plantation along the River Road. It would have been a sizeable distance from the scene of Lucius's rescue in Cobbville, halfway to McRae, Georgia. It seems preposterous to think that Ben could have crossed the river at the ferry and made his way to the marshals before they reached Jacksonville. However, since other men from Irwin County were arrested, it is at least possible that he and the other men were visiting relatives in Telfair at the time. Ben bought a plantation across the river in Telfair the following year. He might have still owned a portion of his family's old home place or he may have been there scouting his prospective plantation. Perhaps he was in Telfair at the time, but there is no record of him being involved in the mob that freed Lucius.

Nevertheless, federal marshals in search of George Morris Williams came to Dickson's Mill and arrested Ben Williams, along with several others in the community. Despite a total lack of evidence supporting his involvement in the mob that freed Lucius, the officers held Ben for two days until they were able to convince others who were involved in the mob that freed Lucius to turn themselves in. Among these were several Fussells, T. J. Williams, Dan Kelley, Dave Wells, Mose Williams and George Morris Williams.[24]

The main argument today for Ben's innocence is the general outrage in his community over his arrest at the time, as well as the fact that the marshals themselves conceded that he was obviously innocent. The article describing his arrest in the *Macon Telegraph* characterizes him as "one of the most prominent and highly respected men of Irwin County" and later notes that "the only connection Ben Williams had with the case was to try to effect a settlement of the trouble between the Dodge Company and L.L (Lucius) Williams. He has the respect and friendship of all the best people of Irwin and Telfair counties, and the Dodge Company will find that their cause has been greatly damaged by the unwarranted action of the marshal toward him."[25]

My grandfather Barclay used to contend that the issue between Lucius and the Dodge Company had already been "settled" by the time of Lucius's murder. This article seems to confirm that a settlement had at least been attempted and that Ben was responsible for it, as does an article published after Lucius's murder. The article contends that Lucius had effected "an amicable settlement" with Captain Phillips of the

Dodge Company and was ultimately willing to go to Macon to face his charges. If true, it seems likely the issue had become personal for Marshal Kelly and Judge Speer in Macon. The Dodge Company was unable to halt the terrible events already set in motion.

The article about Ben's arrest brims with outrage from the citizens, saying that the marshals handcuffed Ben and a man named Tuggins Fussell together "like wild animals," searched his home, and harassed and frightened his wife and children. Indeed, it seems as though the marshals used Ben as bait, holding him until the men for whom they had warrants in Telfair surrendered to them, at which point they released Ben.

If Ben indeed played no role in these events, it seems outrageous that he was arrested and detained with no warrant and held hostage until the actual people under warrant showed up. The citizens' outrage seems justified. If this is true, perhaps the marshals calculatedly captured Ben because of his decent reputation in order to force the others out from hiding and impress them with the marshals' own ruthlessness. One wonders whether Lucius would have responded to such an invitation. Would he have turned himself in to free his nephew? It seems doubtful. He was ready to die for the cause. He probably would have expected Ben to die for it as well.

The marshals' account differs wildly from the newspaper article and contradicts itself in at least one place. The marshals claim at first that after they turned Ben Williams loose, he sent his son over into Telfair County to induce some of the parties to turn themselves in. This was probably C.C. Williams, who would have been 21 at the time. My great grandfather Bunk would have been only 17 years old. Later, they claim that he accompanied them himself. It seems unlikely that Ben would have willingly sent any of his children across the river on such an errand after being freed. What seems more likely is that one of the children traveled across the river while Ben was in custody to inform the guilty parties that Ben would not be released until they turned themselves in. Nevertheless, the marshals admit that they "became thoroughly convinced that he was a good, law-abiding citizen and had no connection whatever with the crimes for which we were making the arrests."[26]

Despite his stellar reputation and his lack of involvement in these crimes, Ben did later prove capable of killing, when he shot and killed a chicken thief at his home in Telfair a few years later in October of 1898. Ben was never arrested nor indicted for this shooting death.

I mention this for no other reason than to point out that even the most "respectable, law abiding citizen" might be capable of killing back then, and a man's right to protect his home and his property was considered absolute by local grand juries and law enforcement. This explains in many ways the central conflict between the "squatters" and the Dodge Company. It proved impossible for the Dodges to legally seize the land of the settlers in local courts. As Cheney portrays in *Lightwood*, the Dodges only recourse was to unconstitutionally move all the land cases, and indeed the murder trial of Captain John Forsyth, into a federal court under their control. The code of the settlers was that a man could and should protect his land with his life. If it was deemed acceptable to kill a man who stole your chickens, then certainly, it was acceptable to kill a man who attempted to steal your home, timber, land, and livelihood. Is it any wonder that the actions of the Dodge Company led to such wanton violence?

Race and Murder

Amazingly, another murder often goes unmentioned in historical accounts of these incidents. It appears that the man earlier "wounded" when the woodcutters on Lucius's son's land were shot at later died. He was a black man named Thomas Young, and T. Jack Williams (Lucius's son) and Lucius Williams were charged with his murder. As a descendant of Lucius Williams, it troubles me greatly that he would kill an unarmed black man employed by the Dodge Company.

The role of the black men in the Dodge troubles has often been overlooked. The sensationalism of the murder of Captain John Forsyth contrasts sharply with the scant references to the murder of a black wood cutter. The murdered man was just following orders and trying to make a living, and it seems unjust in the extreme both that he lost his life and that his family never received (legal) justice for this loss. Blacks were exploited by both sides in this conflict, and this is one area that Cheney tends to ignore, at least in his first novel.

Here, as presented in *Lightwood*, Cheney again has the action play out against the chief villain of his novel, Zenas Fears (modeled on the historical Ed McRae) who is leading a posse to protect the woodcutters. In this fictional version, one of the members of the posse is killed, and the Ruskins (Williamses) are not running log choppers off their own land. They are coming to the rescue of a neighbor's lands. As I noted earlier, Lucius and his sons were well known for helping neighbors in such a manner, so it seems likely that Cheney was merging several historical events into one in this scene from his novel:

> It was late in May. The Swilleys had stopped some company log-choppers. Then Fears and three of his men came and were running the Swilleys off. They hadn't offered to raise their guns at Fears and were backing toward the brow of the swamp hill, when Jock and his three boys suddenly came up over it and cut down on the posse. They brought one of the possemen to the ground and winged Fears. The bullet took him in his right arm and he

dropped his gun and turned tail. Of course the Ruskins had taken to the trees on them and they had to get cover, too, but it was the first time anybody could recollect Fears running.[27]

Cheney chose to ignore the racial implications of this event in his novel, but I doubt race played into Lucius's calculations anyway. He was a man of his time and certainly was far from colorblind. His family had owned slaves, and he probably did as well prior to the war, but he would have fired upon any man attempting to cut his timber, black or white. The company's role in this cannot be overlooked either. They put the black woodcutters directly into the line of fire. After all the trouble with Lucius Williams, I doubt many local whites were vying to be the ones to cut the timber on his family holdings.

The Dodge Company's decision to cut the timber on Lucius's land while it was still in litigation seems reckless in the extreme and designed to promote a confrontation. The fact that this occurred immediately after the fiasco in their failed attempt to apprehend him for contempt of court also seems like tempting fate. Their decision makes sense only if the company was deliberately inciting Lucius to murder in order to strengthen the charges against him. One wonders if the black woodcutters were made aware of the dangers they faced in venturing onto his territory. And what was one black laborer to the Dodge Company? Nothing to them. Nothing to Lucius either. He probably thought no more of their murder than he did of sabotaging a tram road or forging a coffee pot deed. It was just another blow against the company and a small one at that. And one that he would never be indicted for on the local level. Nevertheless, this event and its ramifications precipitated his flight into the woods.

John Williams and T. Jack Williams (Lucius's sons) were both implicated in the shooting death, but both supplied plausible alibis even though Ben Heaps, the chief witness, swore that both were there. Who really killed the woodcutter? It seems credible that Lucius would have done it, although Ben Heaps' testimony casts doubt on this. Why did he not implicate him? Perhaps Lucius was there, but it was his son's rifle fire that actually wounded the man. In *Lightwood*, Jock Ruskin and his three boys fire down on a posse composed of the company enforcer, killing one of the men and wounding Fears, the enforcer. Fears then swears out a warrant for murder against Jock himself even though he knows that Jock was not responsible.[28] A historian must wonder if Cheney's fictional account is essentially true—that Lucius was not responsible for the death but one of his sons was, and the marshals decided to charge Lucius with the crime anyway out of vengeance.

Cheney then relates the following:

Fears went with a dozen men three times to Jock's place during June, but Jock wasn't there. They tried to catch him in Jacksonville and at old Blockhouse Church. They even tried to waylay him coming home, hiding under the Horse Creek Bridge, but every time Jock knew where they were as soon as they had left McRae headed in his direction, and he knew every move they made afterward.[29]

This seems like a fair although fictional account of the struggle to capture Lucius Williams in the months after his escape and the shooting of the woodcutter. Lucius appears to have gone underground at this point, and the marshal's attempts at capturing him failed. Judge Speer claims he was in the "depths of the river swamp."[30] Others support this. One account notes that he hid out on an island in the river swamp. There are many islands along the Ocmulgee River, caused by "cut-throughs." The river is variable and frequently changes course, breaking through a narrow piece of land during periods of high flooding and creating these islands. One such island is located today across from Yellow Bluff, my family's private boat landing. The island comprises about 100 acres in size and is accessible only by boat even today. It is composed of virgin forest, the timber never having been cut, covered in brush, hardwoods, and palmettos, but thick with deer, turkeys, and hogs. Lucius, properly supplied, could have easily lived on an island like this for some time yet been completely out of reach of the federal government. I suspect federal agents would have a hard time arresting him today if he were hidden out in such a place. Lucius definitely had relatives living along the River Road on both sides of the river. This put him in an excellent position to stay hidden for as long as he would have liked.

The Killing of Lucius Williams

Lucius finally was martyred in his cause in May of 1895. He was shot by Marshall Kelly, which in hindsight, seems inevitable. Lucius's adopted sons' involvement in the murder is more surprising. Lucius had served as a sort of foster father to his first wife's orphaned nephews, Cohen and Bob Garrison, who were also his own great-nephews through his sister Emily. These boys teamed with Marshal Kelly to shoot and kill Lucius on the porch of his own home or that of his son John, depending on which account you believe.

It is easy to understand why Marshal Kelly would have wanted to shoot Lucius Williams, a man who had fired upon him before and attempted to stab him to death. His nephews' motives in the story are harder to discern. Addie Briggs describes them as sharpshooters, "quick to fight" and relates several stories about their daring. She states that the problems between Lucius and Cohen arose because Cohen told other members of the family that Lucius should turn himself in to the authorities, that he would definitely be captured because of the big reward after him. This led to a dispute between Lucius and Cohen in which Lucius tried to kill the boy.[31]

Cheney offers no motive for Cohen's treachery other than bad genetics but describes the situation in the following terms:

> They would have been cold trailing Jock till yet if it hadn't been for that Deacon boy. Tump Deacon was a woods colt, according to those who talked to Micajah, and no blood kin of Jock. Jock had taken him when his ma died, in a pole shack out in the pine wilds. He wasn't bigger than a lightwood knot then, and Jock raised him along with his youngest boy. He was close to Jock and stayed there on the place with him, after the other boys had branched off. There were some who said the Deacon boy was a trap-robber and a cattle-thief and that they knew he was no good before anything happened, but the reputation had never got out on him.[32]

Cheney here merges Cohen and Bob Garrison into one character, but still his fictionalized version accords closely with the historic accounts of Lucius helping to raise the nephews of his first wife. Cohen Garrison may well have been a deplorable human being, but his own account of the origin of the conflict strikes me as the most credible. According to Cohen, Lucius was always "a dangerous character" and "nobody dared interfere with him."[33] Cohen claimed to have bought a piece of land from a man who had bought the land from Lucius, but he concluded that the title was not valid and decided to purchase the same piece of land from the Dodge Company instead. Cohen states that Lucius drew his gun and attempted to murder Cohen, but that Lucius's son John, "knocked the gun aside" and prevented the old man from killing him.

Cohen quotes Lucius here:

> "I'll kill both of them, if I have to take a sack
> of rations and stay in the woods until the moss
> grows on my back six inches long."[34]

Cohen claims he took his uncle at his word and slept in the woods until he was able to help Marshal Kelly arrest Lucius. Cohen has long been regarded as a villain by my own family, a dastardly assassin who murdered his uncle in cold blood, but again his statement here seems credible. If Cohen did forsake his uncle's deed for that of the company, then it seems likely that Lucius would have felt betrayed and threatened Cohen's life. His motive makes sense in light of this threat. At any rate, there is some disagreement as to what happened, but the gist is that the Garrison brothers and Marshal Kelly eventually descended upon Lucius at his swamp camp where some shooting occurred and Lucius got away.

They would be more successful when they later found him asleep at his home. Roy Cowart claims that Lucius was murdered at his own home, but Cohen, who was there, says that it was the home of Lucius's son, John. All the newspaper reports of the time say it was the son's home, but Jane Walker and Chris Trowell believe Mr. Cowart. Reports from my own family back up this claim. The house is still standing today, and it seems likely that Lucius's descendants would know which house it was. The house is near the unincorporated community of Cobbville off a Telfair County-maintained road, alternately known as the Firetower Road or Kinnett's Road. It connects Highway 117 with Highway 441. Traveling from 117 to 441, the house is on the right side of the road, set back in an old pecan orchard, near the Horse Creek Bridge, about 12 miles from McRae, Georgia.

Surprisingly, Cheney's fictional account of the murder is much less sensational than reality and once again features the villain and company agent, Zenas Fears, in place of the federal marshal. Cheney writes:

They came to the field horseback and stopped back of the barn. They were running out from behind it before even Jock's wife saw them. He was lying there asleep on a bench on his front piazza. They drilled him between the ears before he could rise up hardly, though, of course, Fears told around McRae that he resisted arrest.[35]

In reality, it was Marshal Kelly, Cohen, and Bob Garrison who ambushed Lucius at the home and killed him. Like Cheney's fictional version, local accounts claim that Lucius was murdered as he slept on the piazza. The Garrisons claim that they crept up to a small shanty behind the home and ordered him to surrender. They asserted that Lucius rose up from sleeping with his rifle and started backing into the home and that Marshal Kelly and Lucius simultaneously fired upon one another, beginning a lengthy and bloody battle. According to the Garrison version, Kelly hit Lucius in the face with buckshot. Cohen said that he saw the blood splatter on the side boards of the house before Lucius retreated inside. The marshals surrounded the house, firing into the windows and the sides of the building.

Bob Garrison claims that he and Lucius had a shooting duel through a window during the battle. Cohen and Marshal Kelly claim that finally Lucius took them unawares and fired at them from around a corner after exposing his body, at which point they shot him again. *The Valdosta Times* reports that after this final shot "Williams lay for a moment motionless on the ground where he fell and then, reaching for his rifle, crawled to the back steps and attempted to mount the shed, the blood flowing from a dozen wounds and leaving a trail behind him as he crawled. Halfway up the steps, he fainted away from loss of blood."[36]

This rendering is cinematic in nature. Either Lucius was murdered in cold blood, or he fought like Rasputin until his dying breath. Once again, a historian finds it difficult to determine the truth of the accounts. Who doubts that Lucius would have fought to the death if confronted? Or that he was armed? Or that he would have reached for his rifle if he had known his home was threatened? But the marshals' story is filled with holes. These men were later charged with Lucius's murder, so they had every reason to lie about how these events occurred. Also, all three had previously had their lives threatened by this very man. Lucius had attempted to kill Cohen. If Marion Erwin, the Federal prosecutor, who authored *The Land Pirates*, is to be believed, Lucius had tried to stab Marshal Kelly to death upon their previous meeting. And several accounts suggest that he and Kelly had fired at one another from his swamp hideout shortly before this shooting. If these men intended to capture or kill Lucius for the reward money, they would have been prudent to shoot without warning, as it was obvious that Lucius was not going to be taken alive.

Recently, a descendant of Lucius Williams, Dr. John D. Williams, told me an anecdote about the events of that day. Missy Williams, Lucius's daughter-in-law, who was in the house during the shoot-out, had always maintained that Lucius was unarmed and retreated back into the house after being shot on the porch. Missy claimed that she offered him his gun, but he refused saying, "It's too late for that. Get the Bible instead, and start praying." In her account, the marshals were never fired upon, yet they continued to riddle the house with bullets long after Lucius was dead.

On the other hand, Lucius's family and friends had every reason to slander the officers, so their accounts may have been modified to make the deed seem more disgraceful. It does matter from a legal standpoint how this incident occurred. Shooting a sleeping man on his porch is murder, plain and simple, regardless of whether you believe the man to be dangerous.

What is not in dispute is that a tremendous amount of gunfire raged after the initial shooting. Kelly and the Garrison brothers fired 81 shots into the Williams home. Ultimately, I have to conclude that the marshals' story is essentially false. Who believes that a 60-year-old man took a load of buckshot in the face and then held off three armed men for a lengthy period of time, alternately firing at them from the windows of the home and ambushing them from the outside of the building, before finally succumbing to their bullets, still reaching for his rifle as his hot blood spurted onto the ground?

Some combination of the two versions is more probable. It is possible that Marshal Kelly did give warning, that Lucius may have awoken and attempted to fire upon the officers initially, and that he may have survived the initial blast. However, he did not possess superhuman powers, and it seems clear that the marshal and the Garrison brothers continued to fire into the home long after he was dead, a home that contained women and children within it. Either way, their deed was disgraceful, and they deserved to be tried for murder in the Telfair County Courthouse. They were indicted and arrested, but a federal writ of habeas corpus saved them from justice by legal means.

Vengeance

The feud did not end with the killing of Lucius Williams. The Garrison brothers were regarded as the worst kind of assassins by the men of my family, who were out for blood. Cohen fled for his life to Mississippi. Roy Cowart describes the ramifications when Cohen returned a few years later:

> [T]he grandsons of Lucius Williams decided they would kill Cohen Garrison for his das-

tardly act against their grandfather. The men were to draw straws to see who would kill Cohen. Tripp Williams drew the shortest straw and was the one to kill him. Tripp would not do it. Another grandson, Bryant Williams, had the next shortest straw and he accepted the job. On Christmas Eve night, 1903, after a service at the Blockhouse Church near Jacksonville, Georgia, Bryant Williams shot and killed Cohen Garrison as he walked out of the service.[37]

Cowart's account is essentially correct, although the shooting almost certainly occurred on Christmas Eve night in 1902, as reported in the local papers at the time. My great grandfather, Barclay Scott (Bunk) Williams, Sr. attended the meeting where the Williams men drew straws to determine who would avenge Lucius's death, but he did not participate. Lucius was his great uncle, not his grandfather, and it probably felt less personal to him than for others in attendance. Bunk had recently married and had a child, my great uncle Floyd, on August 4, 1901.

My father states that Bunk told him and my grandfather that men with wives were exempt from drawing straws. Bunk, however, attended the Christmas Eve service at Blockhouse Church that fateful night with foreknowledge of what was about to happen. He and his wife Bessie left the service early with little Floyd in tow. Bunk was sensible enough to avoid having his infant child and wife watch a man be gunned to death in a church courtyard on Christmas Eve night. They hurried home in their wagon. Little Floyd would have been 16 months old. Bunk chose the right time for his departure because he and his family heard the shots ring out before they got a mile down the road.

Cheney describes the final event in *Lightwood*:

> One of the Ruskin boys had better luck a Sunday night later that fall. Deacon and his wife and baby had come out of Blockhouse Church after the evening meeting and were standing on the steps. There were church–goers ahead of them leaving, but no one in sight to be suspicious of. Deacon had filled his pipe in church and he handed his wife the baby so he could light it. He struck the match, but never got it lit.[38]

The *Telfair Enterprise* reported:

> When the shooting took place, the festivities around the Christmas tree in the church had just ended and the happy throng of children

and older ones were leaving the house to seek their several homes, burdened with the many gifts they had received and enjoying the pleasures which the joyous occasion had brought. Young Garrison was standing near the steps, just outside the church, when he was shot, and when he was reached by those nearest him, it was seen that he was struck by several shots and perhaps fatally wounded.[39]

Addie Briggs's account includes the most details, although, she like Cowart, gets the date wrong. Her account emphasizes the incestuous nature of the murder and the traumatic nature of the event for the children nearby:

It was Christmas Eve Night in the year 1903. The neighborhood was gathered for services in Blockhouse Church. Cohen Garrison was there, too, along with his small daughter. Beside them sat Leila Williams, five year old daughter of Andrew Williams, Cohen's half brother. After the services, Cohen picked up his child, and with his niece Leila and several other little girls trailing along, he made for the church door. Once he reached the top doorstep, he put down his daughter in order to have both hands free to light his pipe. One shot rang out; and he fell dead amidst a horrified group of children.[40]

The grand jury did not indict anyone for the crime although half the community knew who did it. This was the last gasp in the Lucius Williams saga. The community no doubt felt that the shooting was justified after the terrible overreach and brutal murder of Lucius Williams by the federal authorities and the Garrisons had gone unpunished.

The historical record often fails to emphasize the heinous nature of the violence that engulfed the region at this time. All codes of honor had gone out the window by the time of Cohen's murder. It is worth repeating that multiple sources confirm that the Garrisons and John Kelly fired 81 shells into a home housing two innocent women and an infant child. *The Macon Telegraph* reports that "the marshals continued to riddle the house with bullets after the old man was mortally wounded and lay almost lifeless, soaking in his own blood, never having had any warning and having been given no opportunity to surrender."[41] Judge D.M. Roberts described these events in the following terms:

> [A]n old man disobeyed a summons because he said he did not feel that he could get justice in the United States Court, as he felt assured

by what he had heard that the court was thoroughly prejudiced against him, and for disobeying this summons he was shot to death while he lay sleeping on the front piazza of his son's home.[42]

The drastic overreach of the Dodge Company and the federal marshals who worked in league with them left the settlers feeling that dramatic action was the only recourse available to them. Cheney accurately portrays this theme in his novel *Lightwood*. In the novel, Micajah Corn would never fire upon the villain without fair warning, and when his own son participates in the murder of Captain McIntosh (Forsyth, historically), he feels that their cause had been "whored" out. He is disgusted at his own son for hiring an assassin, paying a man to kill for money, which violates the code of honor Micajah lives by. The killing of Cohen Garrison was in actuality the last shot of the Civil War for the men of the 49 Georgia Volunteer Infantry.

One thing is for certain: once Lucius Williams got clear of Johnson's Island prison, he never intended to go back.

Cheney says of the events in his novel *Lightwood*: "I won't pretend to be unbiased in this war, but I will reveal that I changed sides during my digging into the background, in preparation for the writing."[43] This story was personal for

Cheney due to his father's involvement as an attorney for both sides at various times. It is personal for me as well. Cheney's concerns are my own. These historical events happened in the distant past, but as Marcellus Hightower says in Cheney's later novel, *Devil's Elbow*, "The future is only the past, with a new face on it."

The ghosts of the Squatters War still inhabit the river swamps of the Wiregrass region, and Brainard Cheney's agrarian vision survives in the world surrounding the great rivers of South Georgia. Environmentally and historically, those of us who still live along its banks are allied with Cheney, and we must, like Cheney, lament the tragic death of the agrarian dream for these early settlers.

Notes

[1] Briggs, Addie Garrison. *They Don't Make People Like They Used To*. McRae, Georgia, 1985, 24.

[2] Muster Roll of Company B, 49th Regiment. *Research Online.net*. Web. 27 September 2013.

[3] "49th Regiment, Georgia Infantry." Confederate Georgia Troops. National Park Service. 18 September 2013. Web. 27 September 2013.

4 McPherson, James. *Battle Cry of Freedom*. Oxford University Press, 2003, 845.

5 Ibid.

6 Ibid.

7 Muster Roll of Company B.

8 Briggs, 24.

9 Cheney, Brainard. *Lightwood*. Eastman, Georgia: MM John Welda BookHouse, 2012, 212.

10 *Macon Telegraph*, December 12, 1894.

11 Cheney, *Lightwood*, 2.

12 *Macon Telegraph*, December 12, 1894.

13 *Macon Telegraph*, February 5, 1895.

14 *John A. Kelly, et al., vs. the State of Georgia*. Oral Statement of Judge Speer. Macon Georgia News Print Company, 1895, 656.

15 *Macon Telegraph*, December 12, 1894.

16 *Macon Telegraph*, December 13, 1894.

17 *Macon Telegraph*, December 31, 1894.

18 *Macon Telegraph*, January 31, 1895.

19 *Macon Telegraph*, January 20, 1895.

20 *Macon Telegraph*, January 29, 1895.

21 Cheney, *Lightwood*, 12.

22 Ibid.

23 Ibid.

24 *Macon Telegraph*, January 30, 1895.

25 Ibid.

[26] Ibid.

[27] Cheney, *Lightwood*, 213.

[28] Ibid.

[29] Ibid.

[30] *Kelly, et al.*, 659.

[31] Briggs, 28.

[32] Cheney, *Lightwood*, 213-214.

[33] *Macon Telegraph*, May 22, 1895.

[34] Ibid.

[35] Cheney, *Lightwood*, 214.

[36] *The Valdosta Times*, May 25, 1895.

[37] Cowart, Roy. "Legal Treatise." *The Lightwood Chronicles.* Ed. Stephen Whigham. (MM John Welda BookHouse, Eastman, Georgia, 2012), 219-220.

[38] Cheney, *Lightwood*, 221.

[39] *The Telfair Enterprise*, January 8, 1903.

[40] Briggs, 36.

[41] *Macon Telegraph*, May 22, 1895.

[42] *Eastman Times Journal*, June 28, 1895.

[43] Cheney, Brainard. Foreword to *Lightwood. The Lightwood Chronicles*, Ed. Stephen Whigham, 5.

2.

Ecological Disaster Averted: Brainard Cheney's Agrarian Philosophy

Suddenly the gray mist slunk into the dark of the swamps on either hand, the air cleared, and an azure and opalescent eastern sky announced the coming of the sun. Its approach was calm and steady and limitlessly outspreading. The surface of the river grew muddy brown with glinted facets on it. Trees in the texture of the swamp walls became clearly etched in trunk and bough. And the sky above the eastern wall grew richer in ocher, rose and blue—as an organ swells. Suddenly the red sun-rim rose above the tree-line at the end of the reach and a million suns sparkled from the ripples of the river.

—Brainard Cheney, from his novel *Lightwood*

In 1971, Brainard Cheney returned to Lumber City, in the Wiregrass region of south Georgia, and made a trip back down the Ocmulgee, Oconee, and Altamaha rivers. At the time, Cheney was attempting to gain perspective, both on the historical significance of the rivers themselves for the people who have lived along their banks and on his own literary career. His trip coincided with an exploitative proposal by the Altamaha Basin Commission to turn the three rivers into a twelve-foot-deep, hundred-foot-wide, concrete barge channel, potentially disastrous for the region's environment.

After revisiting the rivers of his childhood, and rereading his own novels, Cheney penned an article entitled "Look-a, Look-a Yonder—I See Sunday, I See Sunday! Or, A Deliverer Delivered." The title is a reference to an old timber rafting song, snippets of which are included in Cheney's second novel, *River Rogue*, and Cheney's conception of the Altamaha River as a deliverer of the people who live along its banks. He states within the article: "A Great River Is [sic] both history and prophesy. The Altamaha, Georgia's largest river, though little known beyond the borders of the state, today stands revealed of a great and perhaps unique ecological destiny."[44] Cheney maintains in the article that "the dramatic terms of the four novels I had written about this country and the rivers supporting it grew out of those drawbacks—variable flow, variable stream bed, massive swamps."[45] These drawbacks of the

47

river, while directly causing much of the tragedy in Cheney's novels, also exert a sort of moral order in which the inhabitants must bend towards the will of the natural world and not allow their own materialism and egotism to dominate their existence.

Cheney's article concerns itself with the manner in which these "drawbacks" of the river redeemed it from ecological destruction at the hands of the Basin Commission. The "swamp-bound, variable, changeable river" had acted, and continues to act, as a natural sewage treatment plant for the waste of the millions of inhabitants of its drainage system.[46] Cheney notes that changing the river into a barge channel would destroy this "natural septic tank," and "the consequent pollution would be disastrous for everybody concerned."[47] At the time of the writing of the article, the proposal had already been quashed. Ultimately, Cheney believed that the deliverer had been delivered both by its drawbacks and by the public outcry against the Basin Commission's proposal. He writes:

> And those symbols of the Modern Age, the concrete dam and the reservoir, have lost their ethical significance. There is surely a poetic justice, if not an inscrutable wisdom, in the circumstance that the old Altamaha that has baffled the engineers—in truth, baffled us all for so many years—should turn out to be the

48

hidden Providence of the health of a million
and a quarter of my fellow Georgians![48]

Clearly Cheney found parallels between this ecological
vindication and the meaning of his own literary career. His
novels celebrate the significance of the natural world and emphasize the debilitating effect of industrialization on not only
the physical environment of the South but on the lives of its
inhabitants as well.

Cheney's literary career was both sporadic and poorly
acknowledged. He spent much of his life deeply engaged in
Tennessee politics. His works are not well known today, but
their value in understanding the tensions and struggles of life
in the post-Reconstruction South is still quite relevant. Wilton
Beauchamp and David Matchen refer to him as a writer "who
has developed sound technique, a controlled and polished
style, and a penetrating insight into the art of fiction."[49]

Cheney's exceptional ability to capture the spirit of life in
the Wiregrass region of Georgia is no accident. His birth in
1900 centered him within the circle of a new class of Southern
authors and the beginnings of a literary movement known as
the Southern Renascence. His later attendance at Vanderbilt
University familiarized him with the tenets of Agrarianism
and New Historicism.

Cheney's rural upbringing precipitated his development of
a sense of the relationship between the land and river cycles

49

and the lives of the Wiregrass settlers. As a child, he witnessed the despoilment of the region by industrialists and profiteers. His novels critique the unfettered capitalism that reigned during and after Reconstruction. Cheney maintains that an exploitative relationship transpired between Northern industrialists and the people and Wiregrass region of Georgia. His novels are deeply influenced by the archaic social system and region of his birth and his preternatural affinity for the natural world, specifically the Altamaha River system and its flood plains.

Brainard Bartwell Cheney was born in Fitzgerald, Georgia, on June 3, 1900, to Mattie Mood Cheney and Colonel Brainard B. Cheney. His family was firmly established in the Oconee/Ocmulgee River area, having lived near present-day Lumber City, Georgia, since 1813. Fitzgerald was a temporary home for Cheney's father to practice law for a few years, but the family moved back across the Ocmulgee River in 1906, returning to Lumber City, an old sawmill town located in Telfair County. Cheney's father was a lawyer and farmer, who grew up on a plantation and fought in the Confederate Army at the age of sixteen. B. B. Cheney had at one time been a lawyer for the Georgia Lumber Company, and Cheney would later utilize documents from this dispute known as the "Squatters War" for his historical novel *Lightwood*.

Mattie Mood, Cheney's mother, was the daughter of a Charleston, South Carolina, physician and a member of the prominent Mood family. Charleston would later figure in Cheney's novels in a remote sense, constituting the location of the family homes of Robbie from *River Rogue* and Lucy High-tower in *This is Adam* with Charleston represented as an antithesis to the vulgar and sometimes violent world of the Wiregrass region.

Cheney's father died when Cheney was only eight years old and left his mother with three children and a 2,100-acre farm and timber holdings to manage. It is questionable whether Cheney's mother could have managed the plantation alone, but a black overseer named Robin Bess helped her, and their commitment and determination made a lasting impression on Cheney's mind. He would later dedicate his novel *This is Adam* to Robin, upon whom the main character, Adam Atwell, is based (along with Poss and to some degree, Uncle Mundy from *River Rogue*).

Cheney graduated from high school in Lumber City in 1917 and enrolled at The Citadel upon the advice of his mother. He left as an undistinguished corporal in the spring of 1919, spent a semester at Vanderbilt in 1920 and a summer term at the University of Georgia in 1924. C. Ralph Stevens, editor of a collection of Cheney's letters to Flannery O'Connor, notes that, between the years of 1919 and 1924, Cheney worked a variety of different jobs: "bank clerk (Lavonia, Georgia), timber dealer (Lumber City), crosstie and timber camp operator

(Wheeler County, Georgia), school teacher and principal (Jonesville, Scotland, and Bostwick, Georgia)."[50]

Cheney maintained lasting friendships with some of his students for the remainder of his long life. In 1983, he wrote to one of his pupils with whom he had recently been united on a return to Telfair County: "I still think of you as a very pretty and well-behaved little girl! You and your brother, Norwood, were both of you so well-behaved and bright! And a great relief, in a school that had more than its share of disinterested children and dullards!"[51]

Perhaps the proliferation of disinterested pupils in the Scotland school precipitated his return to Vanderbilt in 1924. There he took courses under John Crowe Ransom, Edwin Mims, and Walter Clyde Curry. He met members of the Fugitives such as Donald Davidson, Merril Moore, and Andrew Lytle, authors with whom he would later become associated. Unfortunately, he dropped out at the end of the school year when his mother died. He began work as a reporter at the *Nashville Banner* in 1925. In 1928, Cheney married Frances Neel, of Newberry, South Carolina. She had recently completed her B. A. in sociology at Vanderbilt and had also taken courses with John Crowe Ransom and Donald Davidson, who was by then teaching at the University. It was during this period that Cheney developed a lasting friendship with another famous Vanderbiltian, the author and poet, Robert Penn Warren. Warren returned to Vanderbilt from Oxford in 1931 around the same time that poet Allan Tate and his wife, author Caroline Gordon were returning there from Paris. He and Cheney became roommates and lifelong friends.

Cheney's work as a reporter led directly to his deep involvement in Tennessee politics. He served as a political reporter at the *Nashville Banner* until 1942. He served as executive secretary to U. S. Senator Tom Stewart after he left the newspaper. Cheney's disillusionment with politics forced him to retire in 1945, although he returned in 1952 as a speechwriter and public relations officer for Frank Clement, governor of Tennessee. During this stint, Cheney penned Clement's celebrated "How Long, Oh How Long, America" keynote address at the Democratic National Convention in 1956. He later handled public relations for candidates for Tennessee governor in several campaigns, thereby firmly establishing himself as a prominent force in Tennessee politics. In a late interview, Robert Penn Warren said of Cheney that he "knows more about Tennessee politics than any living man, still a close friend, wonderful company."[52]

Cheney also penned several plays, which were presented at both Vanderbilt and off-Broadway in New York, affording him some distinction as a playwright. His *I Choose to Die,* based on the life of Confederate hero Sam Davis, as well as *Strangers in This World,* about the snake handling cults of Tennessee and Kentucky, are some of his more celebrated plays.

Cheney's home in Smyrna, Tennessee, known as Idlers' Retreat, became a gathering place for literary figures. He and his wife Francis were enamored of the exciting literary atmosphere at Vanderbilt during these early years. His contemporaries, including Warren, Tate, Davidson, Lytle, and Ransom, had published *I'll Take My Stand: The South and the Agrarian Tradition* in 1930, their Agrarian manifesto. Cheney became acquainted with Tate the following year through Warren. Tate's wife, Caroline Gordon, subsequently became a close friend and a literary mentor for Cheney, offering the young writer advice on his early novels.

Cheney and Warren also shared a mutual relationship in that Warren read and advised Cheney on nearly all of his fiction. Warren wrote that Cheney "helped me a great deal on *All the King's Men*," stating that Cheney was "a constant source of information, pornography, and friendship."[53] The Tate's later conversion to Catholicism in 1947 also influenced the Cheneys who converted in 1953, and, inherently, informed Brainard's later fiction as well.

Cheney's intense involvement with Tennessee politics may explain why, as Ashley Brown notes, "he was the least noticed Southern novelist of his generation."[54] His scant publication history includes a series of articles and book reviews, two plays, and only four novels, which successively waned in popularity as they were published. Incredibly, Cheney never attempted a novel on Southern politics, a subject with which he had become increasingly familiar and disillusioned.

Invariably, Cheney found his subject matter in the rhythms of daily life in the Wiregrass region of Georgia. His novels detail struggles between settlers and oppressive capitalistic systems, exploring the moral systems of both groups. *Lightwood* (1939) and *River Rogue* (1942) essentially chronicle different aspects of the Squatters War between the settlers of the Wiregrass region and the Northern timber companies in the post-Reconstruction period of the late nineteenth century. His later novels, *This is Adam* (1958) and *Devil's Elbow* (1969), were part of a planned trilogy, strongly autobiographical in nature. The two final novels discuss the Wiregrass region during the early twentieth century, after the waning of the timber industry and the rafting traffic along the rivers. The third volume in the trilogy, *The Quest for the Pelican*, was never completed. These novels reflect Cheney's conversion to Catholicism as well as the collapse of Cheney's dreams of an ideal society, a collapse precipitated by his disillusionment with politics. Land battles play prominent roles in these novels as well, as much of *This is Adam* and *Devil's Elbow* are devoted to the widowed Hightower family's attempts to retain their lands in the face of trickery by Northern investors and local profiteers.

Cheney's preoccupation with the ideals and the spirit of the Wiregrass region is not arbitrary. His family had lived in the region since 1813. His father was directly involved in the

Squatters War detailed in *Lightwood*. As Cheney states in his Foreword to the second edition of *Lightwood*, his father had at one time worked as legal counsel for the Dodge Company and even resided in the home of John Forsyth, the historical basis for Ian McIntosh, the company agent murdered by the settlers in that novel.[55] Cheney gained access to the legal records of that conflict through a cousin, and self-admittedly, changed his views regarding the conflict after reading his father's records. He found that his father, too, had changed sides in the conflict, actively representing settlers against the Georgia Lumber Company towards the end of his life. Perhaps due to his family's involvement in these troubles, Cheney maintained a consistent interest in Telfair County politics until his death.

He and his wife's long-lasting correspondence with Flannery O'Connor demonstrates the amount of attention he devoted to local concerns in that she was in the habit of acquiring local papers and sending them to the Cheneys in Tennessee. His concern over political corruption in Telfair County is demonstrated through the correspondence between the two authors:

> I've been having bits of news about the Lumber City difficulties with the Telfair County ring for some time. But I'd heard nothing of this latest incident. The sheriff is supposed to

head the ring (and has for 25 yrs.) and be the chief bandit. Recently the rather simple son of an old friend of mine (now dead) was offered on altar [sic] of the ring's security.[56]

Cheney clearly believed the political environment of Telfair County to be hopelessly corrupted. This passage is in reference to Cheney's "simple" friend going to jail in lieu of the county politicians when the group got into trouble with the FBI for "padding the voting rolls."[57] Obviously, such a revelation did nothing to change Cheney's mind about politics. He finds the same corruption in rural Telfair County that prevails at the state and national levels.

Cheney maintained a close relationship with the Telfair County community all of his life. His father and his mother, Mattie Mood Cheney, are buried at Riverside Cemetery on the outskirts of Lumber City, Georgia, along with three of their other children.

In 1982, Cheney attended the cast off of Project RAFT (Restoring Altamaha Folklife and Traditions), a series of folk festivals held along the banks of the Altamaha and Ocmulgee Rivers between Lumber City and Darien. The main event of the festival was the launch of a 50-ton, 35-by-80-foot raft, and the reenactment of rafting the timber downriver to the port city of Darien. At age 81, Cheney served as a crew member on this vessel, manning the oar. The festival sponsored a reprinting of his timber rafting novel *River Rogue* and renewed an interest in his first novel *Lightwood*, reprinted shortly thereafter as well. Within these novels, Cheney "sought to celebrate the story of the Altamaha and its people."[58]

In *Lightwood*, the aptly named "Corns" embody Cheney's idealized Agrarian vision, and the novel explores the virtues as well as the fragility of their way of life. Its characters exemplify the ideals of the Nashville agrarians. Too simple a way of life to sustain, however, this agrarian idyll is destroyed by a coincidence of internal and external forces. State laws regarding land ownership and traditional "common law" possession and simple codes of personal honor collapse before the apparently impersonal force of federal law, corrupted by northern money and influence. Economic disparity and unfettered capitalism (evident in absentee landlords) transform the land into a commodity to be exploited, not a space to be inhabited. Mechanization encourages this exploitation as the longleaf timber of the region vanishes before the settlers' eyes. At the same time, the poverty and insularity of these "squatters" leaves them vulnerable to greed and violence.

In the novel, the prosperity that the Coventry Company promises to bring to the region never really materializes. All of the land cases are eventually bundled into one, and the company takes all, regardless of title or the worthiness of the claim.

Similarly, in *River Rogue*, one witnesses a parallel exploitation, simultaneous with that of *Lightwood*, in which a specific and insular worker class of the region, the Altamaha raftsmen, faces the same oppressive forces. These raftsmen lead an agrarian existence based on natural river and timber cycles, an existence analogous to the agricultural lifestyle of the Corns, yet still distinctly Agrarian. Within the world of *River Rogue*, and indeed late nineteenth and early twentieth century Darien, Georgia, a monopolistic timber market exploits the raftsmen. The principal buyers in this novel share the name Coventry with the timber company in *Lightwood*. Both are modeled on companies owned by the Dodge family of New York, the Georgia Land and Lumber Company, and the Dodge-Hilton timber company of Darien. Instead of overt efforts to remove the land in question from the settlers as in *Lightwood*, in *River Rogue*, one encounters subtle efforts to defraud the raftsmen in the form of political corruption and monopolistic practices by the company owners. These owners are prominent political figures in the town, transplanted Northerners, often European educated, whose interests are directly antithetical to that of the raftsmen. The raftsmen, like the squatters in *Lightwood*, are powerless before the company.

This is Adam, while remaining in the Wiregrass region, and discoursing once again on issues of Northern exploitation of Southern settlers—this time a prominent Charlestonian widow and her children—is set in a slightly later time period. For the first time, Cheney truly addresses issues of racism and questions as to the future of African-American life in the New South. Adam Atwell himself, the main character of the novel, symbolizes the idyllic agrarian lifestyle, which Cheney portrays as Edenic through the use of Biblical imagery. Adam recalls the Biblical

Adam, and the action of *This is Adam* can be said to occur after the fall. Adam has been forcefully expelled from the garden through the degeneration of an inherently flawed social system. This allegorical reading stretches only so far. Adam is not responsible for the fall; he is not guilty of original sin. The Southern slave culture was doomed, and the repercussions of the Civil War and Reconstruction are visited upon Adam and the other African-Americans in the novel in a far more brutal manner than upon the white characters.

Devil's Elbow is Cheney's only distinctively modernistic text. Within this novel, the land troubles of the region take a back burner to the fragmentation of identity and the meaninglessness of life in the modern world. The tragedy of the earlier novels has been replaced by an absurdity that guarantees nothing:

> It was like looking for your lost memory in another man's mind. Tonight he [Marcellus Hightower] could hear the muddy Oconee laughing. It was windy cold laughter. That ever-moving, deceptively-yielding yellow back, three hundred yards wide and thirty feet deep—yielding nothing.[59]

Here the river becomes a metaphor for the absurdity of modern existence. Marcellus is only redeemed at the end of the novel in a scene reminiscent of the end of *This is Adam*, in which he and his estranged wife undergo a religious affirmation and find solace in God's word, closing out the novel and Cheney's literary career.

So, why have Cheney's novels not received more notice? The Agrarians as a group have received little attention in recent years. Literary critics often contend, somewhat correctly, that the Agrarians' ideas have been "debunked," perhaps even discredited. This constitutes one of the chief reasons that Brainard Cheney has not been "rediscovered" on a national level, like other regionalists from the 19th century, such as Charles Chesnutt. Modern critics by and large display no interest in an obscure member of a faded, debunked, purportedly racist group of long dead white men from the South.

The Agrarian manifesto, released in 1930 and entitled *I'll Take My Stand*, included a series of essays by men of letters from the South. Most were affiliated with Vanderbilt University in one way or another. It included essays on race, politics, education, segregation, industrialization, and the arts.

The Agrarian vision for the nation expressed in *I'll Take My Stand* is unworkable in practice and contains many dated notions about race, economics, education, and politics. Many of the original Agrarians changed their own minds about these issues as the 20th century rolled on. The critic Louis Rubin summarizes the criticism of this movement thusly—that it has often been considered a "misguided, romantic attempt to re-create an idyllic utopia that never really existed."[60] But he goes on to suggest that the Agrarians were aware of this at the time. They realized that their vision of the Old South as an idyllic utopia was false in many ways. Brainard Cheney clearly recognized this as well. The lifestyle of the Corns prior to the arrival of the Dodge Company was far from utopian. Life was brutal in the Old South, most obviously for blacks under slavery but for whites as well. Violence and disease was rampant. The removal of the Native Americans amounted to genocide.

The Agrarians knew this, and they were not advocating that 20th century American society regress to that of the South during the 19th century. They believed that industrialization was not an end unto itself and that industrialized America had lost a sense of environmental awareness, prostituting its connection to the land. Micajah Corn's relationship with the Sugar Field, Adam Atwell's relationship with the Wyche Field, and Ratliff Sutton's sense of peace fishing on the oxbow lake at Longpond on the Oconee are perfect examples of this ideal.

The Agrarians saw "in the history of their own section the image of a region which has clearly resisted the domination of the machine."[61] Cheney differs with them there, in a sense, as he recognizes that in many areas of the South the domination had already occurred. By the time of their manifesto, the rape of the Wiregrass region of Georgia was already complete, and Cheney documents the machine's domination of the region and the collapse of this earlier agrarian idyll. The fact that the Agrarians knew their vision was doomed is clear in Cheney's novels. He essentially records the loss of this ideal. However, this loss in no way diminishes the relevance of his novels for modern readers.

Years after penning his essay "The Briar Patch," essentially a defense of segregation in the South, Robert Penn Warren changed his mind and became a vocal proponent of integration. John Crowe Ransom and many of the Agrarians were later critical of the movement they founded, and they recognized that their views on many of these issues were outdated. The South ultimately did not follow the lead of the Agrarians, and it is perhaps wise that it resisted their initial rebukes. Like the North, it devoted itself wholly to industrialization. The Rust Belt of the North has given way to the Sun Belt of the South. Atlanta, Charlotte, and Raleigh, among other southern cities, have risen from the ashes of Reconstruction and the Civil Rights era. Millions of immigrants from the North have flocked to these cities, as traditional centers of industrialization in the north succumb to decay and ruin. Most modern Americans, as I do, view the rise of the New South as a positive force. The Agrarian dream is dead.

Or is it? I contend that the very element of agrarianism which has survived is the same element on which Cheney focused: the despoilment of our natural resources by unfettered capitalism. In this sense, Cheney is more relevant than ever. In fact, his relevance grows every day. The Agrarians were in many ways a political group. Most of them identified politically as Dixiecrats. They specifically outlined plans for the Democratic Party in their signature work.

John Crowe Ransom expressed his vision that rural New Englanders, farming Midwesterners and Southerners could redefine the Democratic Party as "agrarian, conservative, and anti-industrial."[62] In this wish, he recalls the earlier political philosophy of Thomas Jefferson. His wish and Jefferson's vision have obviously not come to pass. Ironically, he states: "No Southerner ever dreams of heaven, or pictures his Utopia on earth, without providing room for the Democratic party."[63]

What would Ransom and others have made of the Dixiecrats switching allegiance to the Republicans in the 1970s, 80s, and 90s? Most were dead by this time. Cheney lived through these years, but his political views towards the end of his life are unclear. These men were, after all, deeply conservative on states' rights, federalism, education, civil rights, and a host of other issues. One can imagine John Gould Fletcher or John Donald Wade cheering on the candidates for the Republican primary in 2012 who wanted to eliminate the Department of Education. Indeed some of the more radical views of the modern Republican Party come directly from the conservative political philosophies of the Agrarians, who like many members of the modern Republicans, trace their views to the political philosophy and agrarian vision of Thomas Jefferson.

The resurgence of some of the more conservative views of the Agrarians among modern Republicans alone is enough to indicate their relevance today. However, the modern Republican Party would be a far cry from a perfect fit for the Agrarians. The often reckless Republican attitude towards industrialization and commerce for the sake of commerce would have appalled them. The Agrarians would have supported conservation efforts of our natural resources. Cheney certainly thought of himself as an environmentalist. In his 1972 "I See Sunday" essay, he clearly sides with the "environmentalists, ecologists, and fishermen" against the Altamaha Basin Commission and the "regional chambers of commerce."[64] Also, it is interesting to note that Cheney's nephew, Roy Neel, served as chief of staff for former Vice President Al Gore, a noted environmentalist.

It is easy to speculate where Cheney and other Agrarians would side in regards to modern environmental concerns about climate change or hydraulic fracking to extract oil and natural gas. More difficult to imagine is that a group of men who railed against industrialization's "unrelenting war on nature" and man's desire to "conquer nature to a degree which is quite beyond reason" would be in favor of such proposals.[65]

Their conservative ideals may have led them to distrust efforts by the federal government to regulate such issues, but the men who warned that industrialization leads to "overproduction, unemployment, and a growing inequality in the distribution of wealth" sound more like 21ˢᵗ century liberals than 21ˢᵗ century Republicans.[66] They would, however, have hated the word "progressive," so it seems unlikely they would find a welcoming place in either political party in modern America. Their politics and philosophy were complicated, and it is misguided to state unequivocally that they have been debunked and are no longer relevant.

In the 1930s, at least, they favored segregation and settling almost all issues on the local level. They opposed unfettered capitalism to a remarkable degree. In general, they opposed dams and reservoirs and any and all mechanization of natural resources. Mountaintop removal for coal mining would not have appealed to them. Preserving wild rivers would have. Sustainable living would have. The local food movement would have pleased them greatly, as would the new movement toward preserving heirloom varieties of crops and attempts by environmentalists to resurrect these strains that have been thought extinct for many years. The destruction of the 20ᵗʰ century pig farmers by a monolithic giant like Smithfield would have horrified them. Genetically modified crops created and patented for profit by a huge firm like Monsanto might have seemed like something from a dystopian science fiction novel.

Where does Brainard Cheney fit into all this? He was a firm proponent of the agrarian vision. He believed, as did the Agrarians, that "Man [...] is a fallible, finite creature" who is "losing contact with the natural world [...] his machines were brutalizing and coarsening him, his quest for gain blinding him to all that made life worth living."[67]

The introduction to *I'll Take My Stand* states the following:

> Religion is our submission to the general intention of a nature that is fairly inscrutable; it is the sense of our role as creatures within it. But nature industrialized, transformed into cities and artificial habitations, manufactured into commodities, is no longer nature but a highly simplified picture of nature.[68]

Cheney's submission to this concept is most notable in his "Look a Yonder, I See Sunday" essay. The comparison between Cheney's concerns about the proposed damming of the Altamaha River and the already completed damming of the Tennessee River are inevitable, and I believe one can favorably compare Cheney's concerns with those of his friend Donald Davidson in his two volume history of the Tennessee River, *The Tennessee*.

The point of Davidson's much lauded historical work is to celebrate and document the history of the river, while mourning the successful efforts by the Army Corps of Engineers and later the TVA to turn the Tennessee into a "chain of lakes, formed by the impounding of river waters behind great dams."[69] According to Cheney, the point of his (Cheney's) four novels has been to "celebrate the story of the Altamaha and its people [...] the revelation of the river as deliverer, now delivered."[70]

Cheney clearly had in mind his close friend Davidson when he celebrated the delivery of the Altamaha from a similar fate to that of the Tennessee. Davidson describes the Tennessee as "a man-made river, the product of engineering operations of such calculated daring that the imagination is daunted to find precedent for them." It is a "shining modern thing" and "an object of supreme interest to all who want to learn how to control the waters of a river valley and how to convert the force into electrical energy, while achieving at the same time material benefits which are thought not to be readily attainable by other means."[71] Davidson believed that they are attainable by other means.

Davidson begins his work by noting that there are now two rivers. One is the artificial chain of lakes constructed by man, but the old Tennessee yet exists. It is "the river of the Cherokee Indians" though it is lost "beneath the stairs" of this new river.[72] Similarly, Cheney notes: "It is perhaps unknown to many citizens of Atlanta that the Altamaha rises under its pavements in three small streams, to become, before they reach Macon, the Ocmulgee."[73] Both rivers are hidden, at least at their source, by the progress of man, but while Davidson is mourning the exploitation of "his" river, Cheney is celebrating the "delivery" of the Altamaha from the same fate.

Davidson in his first volume prizes the old Tennessee for being the "least friendly to civilization" of all the rivers east of the Mississippi. It "defied every attempt at conquest" and remained "a wild river, cherishing its wildness while civilization rushed across it or away from it." This river "threw back man's improvements in its face and went its own way, which was not the way of the white man."[74]

Cheney feels the same way about the Altamaha, laughing at the earlier failures of the industrialized world to exploit the river. The river's drawbacks had saved it now twice. The variable flow caused the failure of the original industrial exploitation of the Georgia Lumber Company on the Little Ocmulgee back in 1844, and now more than 130 years later, these same drawbacks had delivered it from the exploitative proposal by the Army Corps of Engineers.

Cheney discusses the old days when sturgeon spawned in the Oconee and his ancestors harpooned them for the oil, throwing away the caviar which they had never heard of. He discusses his inclusion of this incident in his novel *River Rogue*. He then points out that when crossing the highway to get to the boat landing in Lumber City on his recent trip down the rivers that he was nearly run over by a "diesel truck, highballing it along the interstate at sixty miles an hour with a load of thirty-foot-long pine saw logs on it!"[75] This is not progress in Cheney's vision. He muses about whether the "ecological future" of the Oconee will return the sturgeon to spawn.

He discusses Gray's Landing, a wild place where he once found himself covered with fleas on his first rafting trip 40 years earlier but which is now "a covered concrete-walled marina with a dozen power boats in it" with "music blaring forth over loudspeakers" coming "from some unseen source."[76] The river is already in many ways alien to Cheney, despite the fact that the proposal has failed.

The trip down the Altamaha River by Cheney and his friend, John Mobley, mirrors in many respects the ending of Volume II of Donald Davidson's book about the Tennessee River. In both instances, the authors return to the rivers of their childhoods, but Davidson's ending is much more tragic. Cheney finds his old landmarks often covered over with freshly poured concrete and sporting goods and grocery stores and playgrounds, but Davidson finds that everything is gone. Devil's Elbow is still on the Altamaha, but Muscle Shoals and the great Suck of the Tennessee have ceased to exist entirely, submerged underneath many feet of water. Davidson's trip is a funeral dirge, ending with the words, "Fare you well, Tennessee," while Cheney's is clearly a celebration. The sturgeon of the Oconee are gone, as are the mussels of the Tennessee, but Cheney's vision has the Altamaha system reclaiming its rights and returning to its natural order.

His novels celebrate that natural order, and his vision grows more powerful each day. All of Cheney's novels are distinctly agrarian in their emphasis on the importance of land and nature in the values of the settlers. Mark V. Malvasi writes the following of John Crowe Ransom's "agrarian aesthetic":

> The southern tradition, Ransom contended, possessed an old and inviolable distrust of rationalism, science, and technology, which, under present circumstances, might remedy the dehumanizing tendencies of the modern world. The social relations of an agrarian society, instead of permitting men the luxury of an illusory power over nature, continually reminded them that their lives were contingent upon the good offices of the Lord.[77]

The tragedy of all four of Cheney's novels rests on the characters' abandonment of either God or the natural world for this "illusory power over nature," a force which ultimately proves to be dehumanizing. Ratliff, in *River Rogue*, like Calhoun Calebb in *Lightwood*, allows his greed to supersede his love of his fellow man. Ratliff's minor redemption in the novel comes only through his return to the Oconee River and the agrarian lifestyle of his childhood. Similarly, Adam Atwell allows his hatred of Oswald Paley to consume him and obscure what is really important—"God's freedom."[78] The crucial scene in *Devil's Elbow* occurs when Sheila withdraws from Marcellus, stating "But you're not religious. And you can't be. You don't believe."[79] His later redemption comes, somewhat problematically, at the hands of a partial religious conversion and his reuniting with his wife, Melanie.

In Cheney's works, tragedy engenders humility. The first two novels are not entirely dependent upon religious conversion. In fact, the conversion of Micajah Corn in *Lightwood* not only fails to redeem Micajah, but also precipitates the downfall of his own way of life. This conversion betrays his own ideal and leaves him emasculated and unrecognizable: a shadow of his former self. In this sense *Lightwood* is the darkest of Cheney's novels and the most tragic. In *River Rogue*, Ratliff Sutton does not accept God at the end of the novel but reacquires his respect for the natural world and an awareness of his own dehumanization, an inevitable consequence of his betrayal of the raftsmen and the river and his rise in the timber industry of Darien. In this novel, God and the river are identified as one. Both require constant humility, as drowning is a constant threat in the novel. Ratliff loses his best friend Poss to the river directly because of Ratliff's lack of respect and humility when he recklessly heads out on a rising river, not heeding the warnings of others.

The differences between these early novels and the latter two must reflect Cheney's own conversion from agnosticism to Catholicism, but the differences in religious tone are of minor importance to the major themes in the works. They all criticize modern technological and rational development. They invoke an earlier time and a simpler way of life, governed by respect for the natural world. Occasionally in Cheney, this natural world comes to life, the river sometimes acting as a character. In the "I See Sunday" article, he writes that while in *Lightwood* and *This is Adam* the "river is incidental to the action on its banks."

> In the other two—*River Rogue* and *Devil's Elbow*—the river contributes controlling action, also. Often enough this involves the rivers so-called *drawbacks*. In these stories, moreover, the river becomes a moral force and mythopoeic stimulus. In *Devil's Elbow* the river takes on a metaphysical function.[80]

This controlling action comes in the form of the drowning of Poss in *River Rogue* and of Marcellus's friend David in *Devil's Elbow*, respectively. Both Ratliff and Marcellus recognize their responsibility in the friends' drowning. The river has punished them for their lack of respect. This punishment serves to reiterate Cheney's most crucial point—that we as human beings are subject to the whims of the natural world, be it God or providence, and that it is a fallacy to think that technological and scientific development can negate this law. In *River Rogue*, Ratliff recognizes that "there was nothing a man could not lose his right to, that however God created a man, he could throw it away, make himself lower than a hog."[81] Cheney saw no difference in a drunken Bear Ike falling off his raft and drowning in *River Rogue* and the Army Corp's failed plans to dam the river 30 years later. Snake Sutton would have laughed at such plans. In the article, Cheney writes with a wry smile: "I can hear Snake Sutton saying now, 'Yeah, 'bout the time them engineers could get their dams built, the old river would have shed her skin and come up somewhere's else—a new reptile, in another swamp!' "[82] According to Cheney, "the concrete dam and the reservoir have lost their ethical significance."[83]

The United States, and indeed the industrialized world, may soon reach a tipping point in unfettered industrialization. Who among us doubts that we must increasingly rely on more sustainable methods of agriculture, energy production, and industrialization? The overreach may have ended, and we may yet see the great relics of the modern age subside into history and the great wild rivers of the past live again. I know it would please Cheney. I know it would please the Agrarians.

It certainly would please me.

Notes

44 Cheney, Brainard. "Look-a, Look-a Yonder—I See Sunday, I See Sunday! Or, a Deliverer, Delivered." *The Southern Review* 12 (1976), 156.

45 Ibid, 158.

46 Ibid, 157.

47 Ibid.

48 Ibid, 166-7.

49 Beauchamp, Wilton and David Matchen. "The Cheney-O'Connor Letters." *Publications of the Missouri Philological Association* 9 (1984), 78.

50 Stephens, C. Ralph. Introduction. *The Correspondence of Flannery O'Connor and the Brainard Cheneys.* Jackson: University Press of Mississippi, 1986, xii

51 Cheney, Brainard. Letter to Emily Narin. 13 May 1983. From the Library of Norwood Davidson, McRae, Georgia.

52 Warren, Robert Penn. *Talking With Robert Penn Warren.* Eds. Floyd C. Watkins, John T. Hiers, Mary Louise Weaks. Athens: University of Georgia Press, 1990, 362.

53 Ibid.

54 Brown, Ashley. "The Novels of Brainard Cheney." *The Chattahoochee Review* Spring (1998), 56.

55 Cheney, Brainard. Foreword. *Lightwood*. By Cheney. Washington, DC: Burr Oak Publishers, 1984.

56 Cheney, Brainard. "To Flannery O'Connor." 8 September 1961. Letter 138 of *The Correspondence of Flannery O'Connor and the Brainard Cheneys*. Ed. C. Ralph Stevens. Jackson, University Press of Mississippi, 1986. 140.

57 Ibid.

58 Cheney, Brainard. "Look-a, Look-a Yonder—I See Sunday, I See Sunday! Or, a Deliverer, Delivered." *The Southern Review* 12 (1976), 156.

59 Cheney, Brainard. *Devil's Elbow*. Eastman, Georgia: MM John Welda, 2012, 59.

60 Rubin, Louis D. Introduction. *I'll Take My Stand: The South and the Agrarian Tradition*. New York: Harper Torchbook, 1962, vi.

61 Ibid, viii.

62 Ransom, John Crowe. "Reconstructed but Unregenerate." *I'll Take My Stand: The South and the Agrarian Tradition*. New York, NY: Harper Torchbook, 1962, 27.

63 Ibid, 26.

64 Cheney, Brainard. "Look-a, Look-a Yonder—I See Sunday, I See Sunday! Or, a Deliverer, Delivered." *The Southern Review* 12 (1976), 157.

65 Ransom, John Crowe. "Reconstructed But Unregenerate." *I'll Take My Stand: The South and the Agrarian Tradition*. New York: Harper Torchbook, 1962, 7.

66 Rubin, Louis D. Introduction. *I'll Take My Stand: The South and the Agrarian Tradition.* New York: Harper Torchbook, 1962, xxiii.

67 Ibid, xii.

68 Ibid, xxiv.

69 Davidson, Donald. *The Tennessee.* Volume One. Nashville: J. S. Sanders and Company, 1946, 5.

70 Cheney, Brainard. "Look-a, Look-a Yonder—I See Sunday, I See Sunday! Or, a Deliverer, Delivered." *The Southern Review* 12 (1976), 156.

71 Davidson, Donald. *The Tennessee.* Volume One. Nashville, TN: J. S. Sanders and Company, 1946, 5.

72 Ibid, 6.

73 Cheney, Brainard. "Look-a, Look-a Yonder—I See Sunday, I See Sunday! Or, a Deliverer, Delivered." *The Southern Review* 12 (1976), 156.

74 Davidson, Donald. *The Tennessee.* Volume One. Nashville: J. S. Sanders and Company, 1946, 6.

75 Cheney, Brainard. "Look-a, Look-a Yonder—I See Sunday, I See Sunday! Or, a Deliverer, Delivered." *The Southern Review* 12 (1976), 162.

76 Ibid, 163.

77 Malvasi, Mark G. *The Unregenerate South: The Agrarian Thought of John Crowe Ransom, Allen Tate, and Donald Davidson.* Baton Rouge: LSU UP, 1997, 44.

[78] Cheney, Brainard. *This is Adam*. Eastman, Georgia: MM John Welda, 2012, 302.

[79] Cheney, Brainard. *Devil's Elbow*. Eastman, Georgia: MM John Welda, 2012, 226.

[80] Cheney, Brainard. "Look-a, Look-a Yonder—I See Sunday, I See Sunday! Or, a Deliverer, Delivered." *The Southern Review* 12 (1976), 160.

[81] Cheney, Brainard. *River Rogue*. Eastman, Georgia: MM John Welda, 2013, 165.

[82] Cheney, Brainard. "Look-a, Look-a Yonder—I See Sunday, I See Sunday! Or, a Deliverer, Delivered." *The Southern Review* 12 (1976), 167.

[83] Ibid, 166.

3.

Lightwood:
The Death of Micajah Corn's Agrarian Dream

It was like the last breath of dying—expected, inevitable, yet blowing a world to bits. Micajah sucked wind shrilly through his mustache. His eyes jerked and his body trembled. He wheeled and disappeared through the shed-room door

—Brainard Cheney, from his novel *Lightwood*

Brainard Cheney's novels must be viewed through the lens of the history of the region in which they take place. Much of their value lies in their poignant representation of the region and time period. The image of the antebellum plantation consistently dominates the history of Georgia, obscuring events that occurred among the lower social classes and in the post-Civil War era. Few authors have tackled the lives of 19th century South Georgians. Those that have confined themselves to local color anecdotes and tall tales. The relevance of Cheney's work rests on his ability to capture the spirit of life in the Georgia Wiregrass region during the late nineteenth and early twentieth centuries. His focus is on an insular group of men and women, known as squatters, though they are not deserving of the term. The characters are hardy pioneers, many of whom are forced from their lands by the timber company, despite their rightful claims. His vision celebrates the ecology of the region and the squatter's code of honor, while examining the forces that led to the dissolution of that code and the unspeakable violence and tragedy that ended this unique way of life.

This way of life began within the watershed of the Ocmulgee, Oconee, and Altamaha Rivers. The Oconee and Ocmulgee run parallel through most of Georgia before simultaneously making inexplicable turns, flowing into one another, forming the Altamaha, streaming into Darien, and, immediately thereafter, into the Atlantic Ocean. Just over 100 years ago, it was still possible to catch a steamboat in Macon, Georgia, journey down the Ocmulgee to the Altamaha and on to Darien, and there board an oceangoing vessel bound for Europe. Enormous amounts of virgin longleaf pine timber existed along these rivers and attracted the interest of Northern developers after the Civil War. The Reconstruction period allowed these corporations, represented by Coventry and Company in Cheney's first two novels, to exploit the local settlers, taking their land and timber with the aid of sympathetic federal judges, and setting up timber mills on St. Simons, thereby establishing an oppressive and monopolistic timber market.

A distinct group of men emerged from this timber traffic culture. They were hardy woodsmen, both black and white, who lived in the floodplains of these three rivers. They led incredibly insular lives, never travelling more than a few miles from home other than the occasional float down-river on a timber raft to be sold in Darien.

Cheney's first two novels chronicle the "war" between these woodsmen and the Northern timber companies, weaving fiction with history in a manner that is extremely relevant in light of the historical neglect of this "war." His first novel *Lightwood* is perhaps the most historically rooted of the two novels. In it, he recounts with varying historical accuracy the story of the Squatters War between the citizens of Telfair and Dodge counties and the Georgia Land and Lumber Company, covering a period from roughly 1868 to 1890.

In his introduction to the 1984 edition of the novel, Delma E. Presley writes that *Lightwood* is a work of fiction and "it is on this level that it can be most appreciated."[84] This statement is undoubtedly true. The novel's basis in history, however, is indisputable and important to any discussion of the work. Cheney, in his brief Foreword to this edition of the novel, acknowledges the historical relevance of the work:

> The persistent trickle of inquiry for this book over the forty-five years since its first appearance, bringing about its republication, is undoubtedly due to its historical content. It is substantially a pseudonymous history of the South Georgia *Squatters' War*. The enveloping action is largely factual. The dramatic action, I believe, symbolically true of the fate of these last victims of the Lost Cause.[85]

With Cheney's words in mind, one may begin to see that while much of the literary value of the novel stems from Cheney's gift for description, his brilliant use of dialect, and the skillful manner in which he portrays the "fall" of the "squatters," most vividly represented in the character of Micajah Corn, the historical value of the work derives from the novel's symbolic honesty to the spirit of the settlers and the "war."

This honesty to the settler's spirit owes much of its structure to the value system of Micajah Corn. The novel begins inside his mind, and the reader soon comes to identify with his moral system, one inherited from his father, Jere. Micajah's early association of the Yankee sawmillers with the

Yankee army he had fought against in the Civil War clearly sets up the conflict of the novel between the Southern and Northern factions, represented by the settlers and the company, respectively. Micajah's attitude towards the invasions of Coventry and Company represents the attitude of all of the "squatters" on the company's land, though the reader soon comes to realize that they are unfairly described with that term. After learning of the extent of the Company's holdings and their plans to ship timber all the way to Brunswick and Darien via railroads, Micajah reflects on the immensity of their effort:

> Suddenly, and it seemed of its own volition, a picture had come into his mind: an army of blue-coated figures, busy as ants, sweating, bustling, moving big pine logs and heaving them into his wagons. Among the sweating workers other bluecoats with gold-braided sleeves moved, gesticulating with drawn sabers. The mules that drew the wagons were close-clipped and bore the brand *U. S.* on their hips. They drew the wagons up to where the logs could be loaded onto railroad cars—an endless train of cars that disappeared into the distance.[86]

Micajah realizes that this vision is not an accurate representation of the actions of the lumber company. Nevertheless, his vision demonstrates the tendency of the settlers to equate the "company" with the Yankee army they had fought only nine years before. To the settlers, the company seems endowed with resources and capital upon a similar scale with the U.S. government. Micajah can only envision them as "a uniformed antpile."[87] The company's later reliance on federal judges and courts to subvert the will of the settlers, local sheriffs, county grand juries, and Georgia land laws reinforces this theme.

Micajah and his father Jere's conversation regarding the seeming impossibility of shipping timber hundreds of miles in a single day reveals the great discrepancy of power between the two groups. While the agents of the company can easily attend court dates in Macon and Savannah and schedule regular business trips to New York and Canada, it takes the Corns three days to make the forty-mile trip from their home at Cedar Creek to the newly formed town of Lancaster, county seat of Coventry county, named after the owner of the timber company. (The town of Lancaster is an obvious reference to Eastman, Georgia, the county seat of Dodge county, named after William E Dodge, president of the Georgia Land and Lumber Company. The town of Eastman was named after one of the principal founders of the company, William Pitt Eastman.)

Cheney represents another disparity between the settlers and the company in the ecological treatment of the land. Jere cannot fathom the longleaf pine of the Wiregrass region being wiped out. He has witnessed an earlier company try to exploit the timber and fail. The Georgia Lumber Company at Lumber City, Georgia, had found the fluctuating water level of the Ocmulgee River too unreliable to float timber down consistently. The mill had shut down in 1842 after only six years of operation. Jere muses on this and states, "I reckon there'll be a-plenty of pine trees left on the barrens when they're all dead and gone."[88] The ensuing action of the novel proves Jere's logic to be wrong. He had not counted on the power of the company, which brought mechanization to the region on a scale with the federal government. The Coventrys do not rely solely on the variable river to float their timber. They built railways, sawmills, and tramroads right into the heart of the timber forests. The company's rape of the region is total; their land claims, all encompassing. The settlers only cut timber when they need ready cash and the river is agreeable. Micajah himself has made only a handful of timber rafting trips in his life. The Corns cultivate the land and rely upon the benevolence of the Sugar Field to provide for their family. Micajah demonstrates a deep respect for land's natural beauty. On his first trip to Lancaster, he acknowledges the splendor of the trees:

Micajah figured that it was seven o'clock when the sun got up enough to come through the pines, sending slivers of gold through the great trunks that stretched up like the strings of a harp. [...] The sky over Blackshear Trail was green pine boughs, a hundred feet high, or near it. In the sun-up stillness they uttered a faint drowsy swish.[89]

Micajah's description emphasizes the virginal nature of the timber while demonstrating Cheney's gift for natural description. It is significant that Cheney spends so much time describing the beauty of the trees on this first trip that the Corns take in the novel. The land has been changed so irrevocably that modern Georgian readers (even in 1939) would have been unable to imagine the landscape as it was in the late 19th century. The 100-foot tall trees are forever gone now. This disparity between the settlers and the company in their appreciation and treatment of the land underscores the agrarian tone to the novel. The railroad at McRae is a source of fascination and, indeed fear, for the Corns. The son, Littleton, reflects that it was the longest clearing he had ever seen. In a humorous scene, reminiscent of the sometimes farcical travels of the Bundrens in Faulkner's *As I Lay Dying*, the Corns are scared off their wagon by the passing of a train, which "came on, right at them—like a steamboat boiler shot out of a gun."[90]

In one of the funniest scenes of the novel, Cheney describes their fear:

> Micajah yelled something and dived out onto the wagon tongue between the horses. But Littleton did not wait to hear, or see. He hit the ground and bounced up at a run. Jet's eyes caught the flash of Littleton's moving legs and he followed him over the side of the wagon. [...] Hissing, beating, clangor, was exploding at their backs, shaking the ground about them.[91]

These men have never faced this kind of "clangor" before. Mechanization is alien to the Corns. It represents the world of Coventry and Company, a world that Micajah and family have not yet begun to fathom. Unlike Faulkner's treatment of the Bundren family, however, Cheney treats the Corns with great respect and prizes their way of life over that of the company agents. The great tragedy of the novel is the inevitable destruction of Micajah Corn's agrarian lifestyle, representative of the lifestyle of the entire region for nearly a century past.

The novel does not take an objective view of the land war. Coventry and Company are clearly the aggressors in the conflict. They precipitate the tragedy of the novel though their greed and abuse of the power granted them by federal judges during Reconstruction and post-Reconstruction. Cheney firmly establishes the Corn's property rights for the satisfaction of the reader. They are represented as simple yeoman farmers, living in a symbiotic relationship with the land, an existence based on river and harvest cycles. Micajah's reminiscences after his trip to Lancaster establish the Corns as one of the oldest families in the county, having settled the region prior to 1820.[92] Cheney ignores the issue of Native American ownership, as Jere Corn was an Indian fighter himself, having been scalped shortly after his arrival in South Georgia, and possessed of the firm conviction that he won the land he lives on, having fought the Indians for it. The company agents' later references to the Corns as "squatters" seem ludicrous in light of their historic possession of their home place. Having lived on the land for over 50 years prior to the current conflict would seem to securely place the ownership of the land with the Corns.

On their first visit to Lancaster, the Corns encounter their cousin Calhoun Calebb, who helps them locate the company agents in order to discuss Coventry and Company's claims to their farm. Calebb clearly articulates the Georgia law regarding land ownership under adverse possession. According to Calebb, "Twenty years' actual possession, even without color of title, gives a man absolute claim."[93] As in the case of the Corn family who purchased deeds to their holdings during the tax sale of 1845, "the claim becomes absolute after seven years."[94] The Coventry agent, Major Rhea's, initial reply to the Corn's claim is revealing in the response it provokes in Jere Corn. Rhea declares his intention to recheck the company's claim, telling the family, "By the law of Georgia it's yours—it is yours by the law." Jere replies in the dialect of the Wiregrass region: "We don't question it a-bein' our'n—it's our'n all right. By the law of Georgie, aer by the law of shotgun!"[95] The Corns haven't come to Lancaster to clear the title. They have come to resolve any issues with the company before they start.

Jere here asserts his intention to guard his holdings with his life. Through the character of Jere, Cheney celebrates the rawboned spirit of the backwoodsmen, demonstrating a distinct cultural disparity between the Yankee agents and the settlers. When Jere first came to Cedar Creek, the law of the shotgun "was the only law," and he still relies upon the honor and values implied in this law to protect his family and his holdings.[96] The Coventry Company does not play by the same book of rules. The ruthlessness of the land agents ultimately precipitates a brutal response from the settlers, who, in Micajah's view, eventually lose sight of their honor and values as well. The loss of these cultural and moral values, passed on from Jere to his son, Micajah, constitute the heart of the conflict and the tragedy of this novel. The eventual loss of the Agrarian dream during the novel rests upon the failure of the characters involved to adhere to this code.

Caught somewhere in the middle of this settler-agent/Southerner-Yankee continuum is Calhoun Calebb. Much of the book is presented through his point of view; he and Micajah Corn share the title of "main character." Calebb, however, does not really fit in with either side in the novel. Cheney bases this character upon the real life lawyer, Luther A. Hall, of Eastman, Georgia. J. N. Talley writes the following of Hall: "In early life he was the victim of an unfortunate accident, which left a cheek scarred for life, and a sightless eye, over which he wore a green shield. He had been a school-teacher, was a lawyer of ability and skillful in ejectment practice."[97] Hall loomed larger than life, historically and physically. He was supposed to have stood well over six feet tall, weighing over 300 pounds.

Cheney's character, Calhoun Calebb, is faithful to this description. In the novel, Calebb's physical disfigurement, along with his half-Yankee, half-Southerner heritage, chiefly influences his actions and status. More than anything else, he resembles a "grotesque" out of a Flannery O'Connor novel. One can note elements of Southern Gothic and psychological realism in Cheney's style, especially in his approach to Calebb's character. Calebb derives much of his motivation in the novel from revenge over torment he received as a child for his disfigurement as well as the occasional ostracism he receives as an adult from respectable Lancaster society.

Calhoun reflects that his memory does not go further back than the burn he received in his fifth year. His memory since then is one of cruelty and name-calling. The other children in his school refer to his father as a "damn Yankee runaway," while labeling Calhoun *"Cutplug"* and *"Rawmeat."*[98] These psychological wounds lead Calebb to wicked and self-destructive acts, foreshadowing his later role in the assassination of Captain McIntosh. As a child, he particularly could not stomach the pity of Fulmer Grainger and repaid his kindness by throwing him from a steamboat and nearly drowning him, earning Calebb ostracism from the other children. The Civil War, however, changed Calhoun's status. For him the war manifested a redemption of sorts, raising his status by applying the label of Captain to his title. Calebb won respect in the war and he welcomed the ensuing Yankee occupation just as he welcomes the current invasion by Coventry and Company. Calebb expresses this sentiment as he reflects on his friend's near drowning:

> Now he did not mind his disfigurement and nobody cared who his father was—the war had changed a lot of things.
> The war! The war! He thought of its foolish beginnings. [...]But all of that has ended with the war—the ragged, one-eyed war! No more half slave and half free—no more half-breeds!

> Now a new day and a new country—these Pine
> Barrens—with their railroads and sawmills![99]

Initially in the novel, Calhoun seeks to profit financially through Coventry and Company, thinking his relationship with the locals will make him a valuable commodity to the corporation, while reflecting that he and the Yankee owners and agents share a common heritage. Calebb has never abided by the code of the backwoodsmen. Greed and a twisted sense of revenge rather than a true desire to protect the property rights of his brethren motivate Calebb and precipitate his failure and lack of redemption in the novel. After being refused employment by the company, Calebb switches sides, defending the settlers against Coventry's ejection suits for a handsome profit. After winning his ninth suit, Calebb reflects on his success, noting that, "In those early days when he talked about the prosperity Coventry and Company would bring to the Pine Barrens, he hadn't guessed his would come in such a way."[100]

Calebb's prosperity in the ejection suits as well as his conviction that his disfigurement might have influenced the company's rejection of him instills a malevolent sense of revenge in the character, causing him to discard his earlier notions about "shared heritage" with the company agents:

When the Coventrys first came, he had imag-
ined he had something in common with
them—a heritage. What rot![...].He would certainly make common lot with the squatters as
long as he could win their claims in the courts.
A sorry pack of hounds, maybe, but they were
for him and he was for them. If there must be
boot-licking, he preferred to wear the boots.
Nine ejectment suits weren't even an eye-
opener—Coventry's land claims offered vast
possibilities.[101]

Although Calebb's disfigurement and problematic childhood instill initial sympathy in the reader, the revelation that
Calebb's interest in the Coventry land claims is motivated
purely by profit and revenge demonstrates the complexity of
his character, while foreshadowing his later actions in the
novel. The novel invites comparison between him and
Micajah Corn, a character presented in a more tranquil light,
obedient to a just cause, wholly deserving of sympathy. Some
of the novel's tragedy results from Calebb's ability to persuade
the squatters to identify him with their cause. Once they
choose to follow Calebb rather than Micajah, their fate is
sealed.

The reader's sympathy does not extend itself to the company agents. Cheney demonstrates their dishonor and ruth-

less nature in their willingness to proceed in their land claims against the settlers even in cases in which they know the settlers' claims to be valid. Major Rhea objects to some of the company's claims, stating that he knows the settlers in question and recognizes their titles as valid under Georgia law. Coventry Company attorney, Lechleiter, states the opinion of the management in no uncertain terms:

> It is up to the lawyers to supply a plausible theory—that's what the company hires them for. [...]. And as for the Savannah judge, I will tell you now, I have more than a hope for sympathetic treatment. [...]. We can't take a chance on losing a quarter of a million dollars' worth of timber![102]

According to Lechleiter, the company's acquisition of the land depends upon the movement of the land cases to a federal court in Savannah over which the company holds sway. Their later firing of the sympathetic Major Rhea further indicates their desire to take advantage of the settlers.

In light of the company and Calebb's actions, Cheney's representation of Jere Corn's death seems almost merciful. Corn's demise presages the death of an entire culture that he has come to represent. Micajah Corn articulates the passing of this spirit in his thoughts upon his father's deathbed:

Micajah thought, with a smile that rose only to his eyes, that Jere would have wanted to go to Pineville with him, toting his gun—if he'd known. In the late night a crumbling fire in the big fireplace filled the dim room with wavering shadows. Micajah gazing at the vague, muttering old man nearing death in the white bed had the queer notion that he was carrying away with him the security of their past.[103]

The "wavering shadows" represent the fleeting nature of not only human life, but the very codes and systems upon which individuals base their lives. Micajah takes comfort in his father's toughness, his unwillingness to part with his property on any terms. The shadows, however, indicate a temporal quality, a flickering, of which Micajah is also aware. Micajah is thankful that his father will not live to see his way of life destroyed and the land upon which he has raised two generations of Corns stolen by Coventry and Company. He senses that Jere's way of life is dying with him.

Micajah's awareness of his father's nobility along with his desire to pass these traits and values along to his children chiefly influences his actions in the novel. Cheney endows Micajah with subtle nobility in his decision to stand beside the other settlers in the conflict. We first see this nobility when

Micajah attends the trial of Ardel Cone in McRae, Georgia. Ardel married Micajah's daughter against his wishes, and Micajah thinks little of the man or his family. Nevertheless, he and Jet attend the trial. Micajah doesn't speak to Ardel, but he is secretly pleased when Jet reaches out to Ardel without being told. (Ardel Cone seems to be based on Andrew Renew, who was falsely accused of the murder of John Forsyth and shot dead by E.A. McRae).

Later, Micajah faces a similar but more dangerous situation when the company attempts to evict Dan McMillan, another Corn son-in-law. Dan has been threatened by the company's enforcer, Zenas Fears: "Micajah did not reply immediately. He looked out across the cowpen field from the corncrib door where they were standing and above the tree-line at the sky. Then he nodded his head slowly and said, 'Me and Jet'll come, Dan'l.'"[104] Micajah's gaze demonstrates the manner in which emotion and the natural world are connected in *Lightwood*. The cowpen field and the tree-line are signifiers of the Agrarian lifestyle and highlight the need to protect that way of life by fighting the company's aggression. Micajah later feels pride when his son Jet voices a similar reaction: "I reckon we'll have to do something about that, won't we, Pa?"[105] In both instances, Micajah has been successful at passing on his code of honor to his son.

Cheney represents the turbulent nature of the post-Reconstruction era in one of the most gripping incidents in the novel, the race riot in Lancaster and the ensuing murder of David McIntosh. Also historical in nature, this scene reveals Calhoun Calebb's deceitful nature in the way he utilizes the murder to pursue his suit with David's sister, Kathleen.

Gathered in Lancaster for a church revival, a group of several thousand African-Americans erupts into violence after a drunken dispute over a card game results in the death of one of the men at the hands of a white Lancaster deputy. The crowd turns into an angry mob, pursuing an innocent white citizen, David McIntosh, into a local home, after which they drag him out and slice his throat. Here Cheney effectively demonstrates the tensions between white and black settlers of the Wiregrass region in the post Civil War area. Historian Mark V. Wetherington writes of the historical event upon which the incident is based:

> The Eastman riot was much more than a drunken melee that resulted in the death of a Macon gambler and an innocent Cochran boy. More than any other local event it symbolized the transitional nature of Wiregrass society during the 1800s. Railroad construction, which had opened up the forest to economic development, also made its communities vulnerable to less desirable invasions. Liquor was much more available at the depot towns; and

the railroads made possible the arrival of hundreds of outsiders within hours, radically changing—if only for an hour or two—the racial composition of a community.[106]

In this manner, one can see that the lesson of both the novel and the historical record seems to be that industrialization can foster adverse effects on Agrarian societies, that violence often precipitates or accompanies social upheaval and radical change. This incident is also significant in its demonstration that Coventry and Company was not the only agent of change present in late 19th century society. The death of Micajah's way of life was inevitable. The rise of black society, industrialization, and the railroads were all factors.

Using the story of the Lancaster (Eastman) riot, Cheney weaves history into fiction while confirming Calhoun Calebb as a villain. David McIntosh's death eventually results in Calebb's temporary engagement to Katherine, although she later jilts him for John Casement, one of the company agents. Although Calebb, through treachery and manipulation, is able to prevent Katherine and Casement's marriage, he alienates himself from Katherine in his battles against the company, represented in Coventry County principally by her father Ian McIntosh.

Ultimately Calebb's moral and social failure in the novel rests on his perverted sense of vengeance towards the company—and specifically Kathleen McIntosh and her father, Ian. Calebb remains true to neither faction in the Squatters War, basing his hatred on his shame over his failed relationship and disfigurement, a hatred that is wickedly intensified when he hears Kathleen McIntosh make jokes about his appearance in the downstairs of the courthouse. Cheney places great emphasis on Calhoun's physical reaction to the mental anguish and embarrassment he feels:

> Pain thrust up from his cheek through his
> brain. His brain throbbed as if it would knock
> the top off his head. The room grew misty,
> swam before his eye. He vomited.[107]

From this moment on in the novel, revenge and hatred govern all of Calhoun's actions. His later jailing as a result of a lawsuit by the company and the implied election fraud in his failed bid for the Georgia Senate, further fuel his rage. These events are also historical in nature, as the Eastman lawyer Luther A. Hall, after defying a federal court injunction to desist all claims to the disputed lands, was sentenced to five months imprisonment in Chatham County jail in March of 1890 for contempt of court.[108]

Calhoun's dark motives precipitate one of the greatest tragedies in the novel: the murder of Ian McIntosh (historically John Forsyth). He is the one agent of the company, other than the quickly dismissed Major Rhea, who reveals himself to be at all sympathetic to the plight of the woodsmen in Cheney's novel. An article in the *Eastman Times Journal* describes the historical company superintendent as "a thorough businessman" but "the working man's friend" and claims that "every man [in Normandale] will take up for Capt. Jack, as he is called by all."[109] Forsyth/McIntosh's death was far from inevitable, both in history and in the novel. Micajah himself attempts to end the fighting at one point. After Zenas Fears moves to Pineville and leaves another agent in his place at McRae, Micajah discontinues his attempts to sabotage the company, telling his son, Littleton:

> "Now we've got cotton-picking to do. And it's about time you was a-comin' to yore senses and a-takin' yoreself in hand!" He added that the company wasn't bothering anybody around the county now—they had a new man and nobody had been run out of his timber that summer.[110]

While Micajah regards the dispute with the land company as a temporary impediment to his way of life, a diversion from his true work—planting the Sugar Field—he realizes far too late that his children view the affair differently. Fighting the company is all they have ever known. That is their way of life, and they view planting crops as the diversion. Tragically, Littleton goes on a rafting trip anyway, convincing his brother Zeke to help him sabotage a company raft train. Zeke is killed, once again by the villainous Fears. Micajah retrieves his son's rotting body from the swamp and travels 60 miles upstream to bury him. The incident continues the violent land war, leading inexorably to the murder of McIntosh.

The reader realizes that the proper victim, the true villain of the novel, is Zenas Fears, the traitorous local agent and enforcer for the company. His actions are even more heinous in light of the fact that he is a local and knows these settlers' claims to be valid. Cheney based Fears on the character of E. A. McRae, who served as company agent for the Dodge Company during the events of the novel and later referred to the settlers in a letter to the public as "land pirates [...] whose only title to land was a forged deed and a shotgun."[111] (In this treatise, McRae also falsely asserts that the Dodge's claim is "complete" and "indisputable" and disparages many of the Telfair County squatters by name, including Andrew Renew, whom McRae had personally killed under false pretenses. E. A. McRae was later shot to death, ironically over a piece of Dodge Company land that McRae claimed for himself without a deed.)[112]

Micajah Corn, bearing Fears's treachery in mind after Calebb's failed bid for the State Senate, proposes a violent but, in his eyes, honorable solution before the local Alliance men. Micajah's words are chilling in their severity:

> Two hundred of them [...] would be enough to burn the mill. [...].Hatton could take the seventy-five left and rush Camp Six about the same hour, putting the torch to it. If the other fourteen would ride with [Micajah], saddleback, they would start off now for Fears' home.[...] They needed nothing to make ready, except their guns and twelve feet of rope.[113]

Micajah's proposal, though grim and certainly cold-blooded, follows the law of the shotgun set down by Jere. The burning of the company mill and Camp Six are just punishments for the company by the men whose land the company has stolen. As for the murder, Micajah himself offers to lead the lynching. He suggests that his son, Littleton, and the "Ruskin" boys be the ones to participate. All of these men have had a family member murdered by Fears. Jet and Zeke Corn were both personally killed by Zenas Fears, as was Jock Ruskin.

Calebb thoughtlessly dismisses Micajah's proposal, asking the Alliance men to wait until he can come up with a better solution, thereby alienating himself from Micajah. Micajah responds by losing interest in the conflict and returning to the tending of his fields—the cornerstone of the lifestyle he has been fighting to protect. Micajah throws himself diligently into his farm work, but harbingers of doom disturb his conviction. While fixing a gourd on a pole, he reflects on the nature of his confusion: "There was a whole lot he couldn't figure out of late. It seemed that the older he got, the less he could figure anything out. About man and God! He even wondered about himself, sometimes!"[114]

Micajah's religious uncertainty here prefigures his inexplicable religious conversion later in the novel. This uncertainty gives way to a prophetic feeling, a "token" in which Micajah realizes the tragic nature of his fate: "What was making up? Who was making it? He looked at the tree-line in the distance and at the sky beyond. The threat was there, but he could not say."[115]Micajah's "token" here reveals his own realization that his way of life is dying—that the war between himself and the company has taken on a life of its own, apart from him and his convictions. The misfortune of the novel is that the agrarian lifestyle which the Corns have enjoyed for three generations in the Pine Barrens is ultimately doomed, and the land war with Coventry and Company is secondary to the inevitable decline of the age. Micajah realizes that "the quarrel with the company had not been settled yet.[116]" Yet he also realizes the intangible nature of the "threat" that manifests itself along the horizon in this scene. It is "clouded up" and impossible to grasp.

Calhoun answers Micajah's question through his subsequent plotting of the murder of McIntosh without Micajah's knowledge. Calebb, along with Sheriff Mathias Hurd (based on Wright Lancaster), and Micajah's son, Littleton Corn, conspire to hire a black man named Trigger Fowler to murder Captain McIntosh in his home. The historical basis for Cheney's character is Rich Lowry, a man known as "the Scuffletonian," of African-American, Native-American, and white descent. In *Lightwood*, Cheney describes Fowler as having a "light" face, "more of a copper-red than yellow and his cheekbones were high."[117] This man's fate is uncertain both in the novel and in history. Lowry disappeared after the murder, but it is thought he was killed by one of his co-conspirators. Interestingly, the Scuffletonians of North Carolina were said to descend from the settlers of the lost colony of Roanoke Island.[118]

Littleton and Fowler commit the murder of Ian McIntosh under cover of darkness, emptying a shotgun through the den window. Calhoun reveals his propensity for evil upon hearing that the murder was a success. He reflects on the local gossip: "*Blew his brains out!* The fire had burned low and Calhoun leaned on the mantel again. And blew her heart out, too! He rubbed his hand over his left cheek."[119] In having Calebb touch his facial disfigurement, Cheney draws attention to the similarity between Calhoun's physical deformity and his mental derangement. The murder of Ian McIntosh benefits neither Calhoun nor his real life counterpart, Luther A. Hall. Both received sentences to life imprisonment in a Columbus, Ohio penitentiary.

Calhoun, as much as Coventry and Company, is responsible for the death of Micajah Corn's way of life. Micajah recognizes the dishonorable nature of the murder and reflects on Littleton's part in the conspiracy: "Carrying his gun to kill a man—*for the nigger to kill a man*, for money! A man he, Littleton, had scarcely ever seen, who had never done him any harm."[120] Micajah rejects this murder for its unscrupulousness. It fails to follow the law of the shotgun, in which murder is permitted only if one has been directly wronged by the victim. Micajah's moral system rejects the principals of murder for hire, but Micajah ultimately recognizes that his dogged pursuit of revenge for all these years has led his son down this path of dishonor and violence. His agrarian vision has been corrupted.

Micajah's resulting anguish over his son's part in the murder, as well as the revelation that Calebb has impregnated his daughter Jasmine, effects a radical change in Micajah, precipitating a stroke and religious conversion. His decision to become a company informant against the murder conspirators, including his own son, is perhaps the most bizarre and unexpected plot line in the novel, though it has basis in history. In

The Land Pirates, prosecutor Marion Erwin gives a vivid description of Lem Burch's confession, which was delivered directly to him and resulted in the immediate paralysis of one side of Burch's body. His later testimony had to be given from a boarding house bedroom near the courthouse. Micajah Corn's character derives from the real-life Lem Burch and other conspirators.

Micajah's change is somewhat bizarre, even considering the incredible stress he underwent and his struggle with his religious conviction throughout the novel. His son Littleton barely recognizes him at the trial, noting that his father "looked strange" with a "dead half of his face that took no part in what he was saying or doing."[121] Micajah strangely cackles at Littleton's penetrating gaze, but his betrayal of his son and countrymen affords him no redemption in the novel, either spiritual, moral, or in the physical form of having his land claims validated by the company. His decision to testify begins the final sequence of the story.

The company's final blow to Calebb and the other conspirators is to have them tried, not for murder, which would result in a local trial with a possibly sympathetic jury. They are charged in the Federal court in Macon for a "conspiracy, unlawfully and feloniously entered into with the object of injuring Proudfitt Coventry because of his previous exercise of rights secured to him by the Federal Constitution and laws of the United States."[122] J. N. Talley writes that the charges in the actual case were "that a conspiracy had been formed by the defendants to injure, threaten, oppress, and intimidate Norman W. Dodge [...]"[123]

Quite obviously, the charges are not faithful to the crime. The defense lawyers point out that Proudfitt Coventry had never even set foot in the state of Georgia, nor had ever been seen by any of the defendants. These charges represent a further injustice by the company and the federal court upon the settlers of the Wiregrass region. The novel does not question their guilt, but it does make it abundantly clear that the defendants' rights to a fair trial have been forsaken. Micajah's testimony seals the defendants' respective fates. They all go to prison, including Micajah's son Littleton. Micajah goes home with false confidence in his decision and in the continued preservation of his way of life, eagerly anticipating the return to his agrarian existence: building a new trough and feeding the livestock.

After riding the train home from Macon to McRae, he wanders into a local eatery to rest and is confronted by a new agent for the company. The man gives Micajah a summons and seals the final tragedy of the novel with his words:

> 'Served eighty-eight of these summonses in the last six days,' he said. He stood a moment with his hands in his hips, rocking back on his heels. 'The company's bundled the whole lot of

land cases into one ejectment suit. They're going to try it in the Macon Court.' [124] Micajah responds incredulously: 'Macon?' he said. 'Macon Court.'

Micajah's confusion here once again draws attention to the disparity between the settlers and the company. Although the star witness for both the company and the government, to the new agent, Micajah is just a number to be "bundled" in with the other cases. His way of life is over, and Coventry takes all of the land. Micajah's disillusionment with a cause perverted by Calhoun Calebb's greed and selfish motivations results in the loss of his last son. Neither the company nor the novel honors his action, and his ultimate fate is the loss of the lands that he has sought to protect. Micajah and Jere Corn's agrarian vision has been destroyed. Cheney's novel illustrates the tragic inevitability of this loss and the lack of redemption both for those willing to change and those who are not.

Critic Ashley Brown writes of Jere and Micajah Corn that the two "live by a simple but deeply felt code of honor; in this post-Reconstruction society they already represent a point of view that was somewhat antiquated, and the final irony of the novel is based on this."[125] Ultimately Cheney's novel details the circumstances of the inevitable death of this code, while venerating Micajah's early agrarian vision and lifestyle over that of Coventry and Company and the industrialized world.

Notes

[84] Presley, Delma. Introduction. *Lightwood*. By Brainard Cheney. Washington D. C.: Burr Oak Publishers, 1984.

[85]Foreword. *Lightwood*. By Cheney. Washington, DC: Burr Oak

Publishers, 1984.

[86] Cheney, Brainard. *Lightwood*. Eastman, Georgia: MM John Welda, 2011, 2.

[87] Ibid.

[88] Ibid, 5.

[89] Ibid, 7.

[90] Ibid, 10.

[91] Ibid.

[92] Ibid, 31.

[93] Ibid, 29.

[94] Ibid.

[95] Ibid.

[96] Ibid, 30.

[97] Talley, J. N. *The Dodge Lands and Litigation: A Report Delivered Before the Georgia Bar Association, June 4, 1925.* Tybee Island, GA: Georgia Bar Association, June 4, 1925, 245.

[98] Cheney, *Lightwood*, 80.

[99] Ibid, 82.

[100] Ibid,77.

[101] Ibid.

[102] Ibid, 89.

[103] Ibid, 99.

[104] Ibid, 103.

[105] Ibid, 104.

[106] Wetherington, Mark. *The New South Comes to Wiregrass Georgia: 1860-1910.* Knoxville: University of Tennessee Press, 1994, 280.

[107] Cheney, *Lightwood*, 243-4.

[108] Talley, 250.

[109] *Eastman Times Journal*, August 23, 1889.

[110] Cheney, *Lightwood*, 235.

[111] McRae, E. A. "A Letter to the Public." *The Dodge Land Troubles.* Eds. Jane Walker and Chris Trowell. Fernandina Beach, Florida: Wolfe Publishing, 2004, 546.

[112] *The Eastman Times Journal*, April 17, 1913.

[113] Cheney, *Lightwood*, 287.

[114] Ibid, 293

[115] Ibid.

[116] Ibid.

[117] Ibid, 291.

[118] Talley, 252.

[119] Cheney, *Lightwood*, 299.

[120] Ibid, 314.

[121] Cheney, *Lightwood*, 340.

[122] Ibid, 329.

[123] Talley, 255.

[124] Cheney, *Lightwood*, 345.

[125] Brown, 57.

Illustrations

Map outlining the area covered in Brainard Cheney's novels

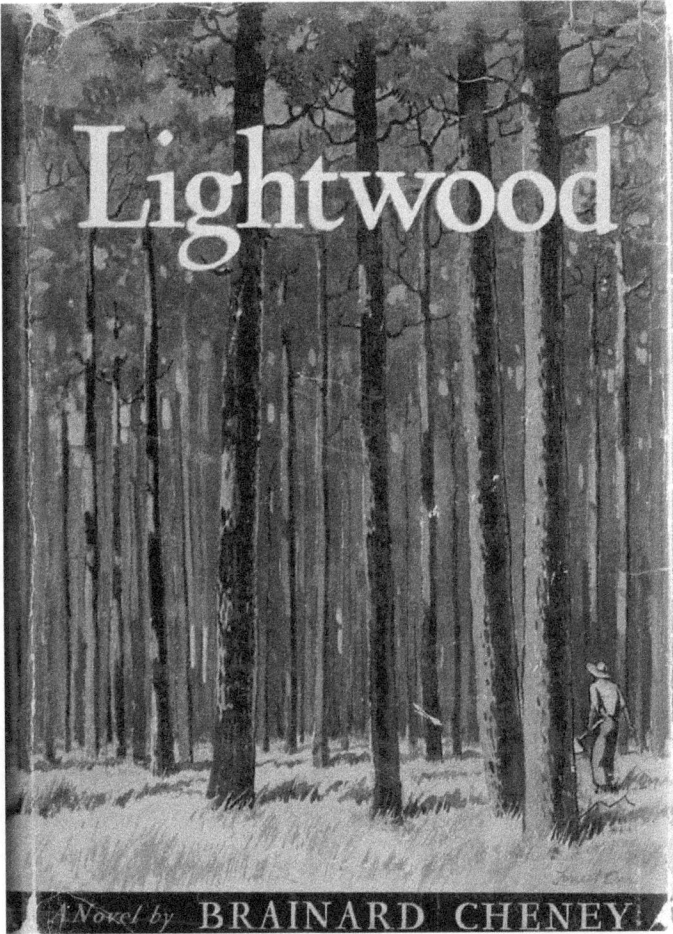

Original cover for the novel, *Lightwood,* published in 1939

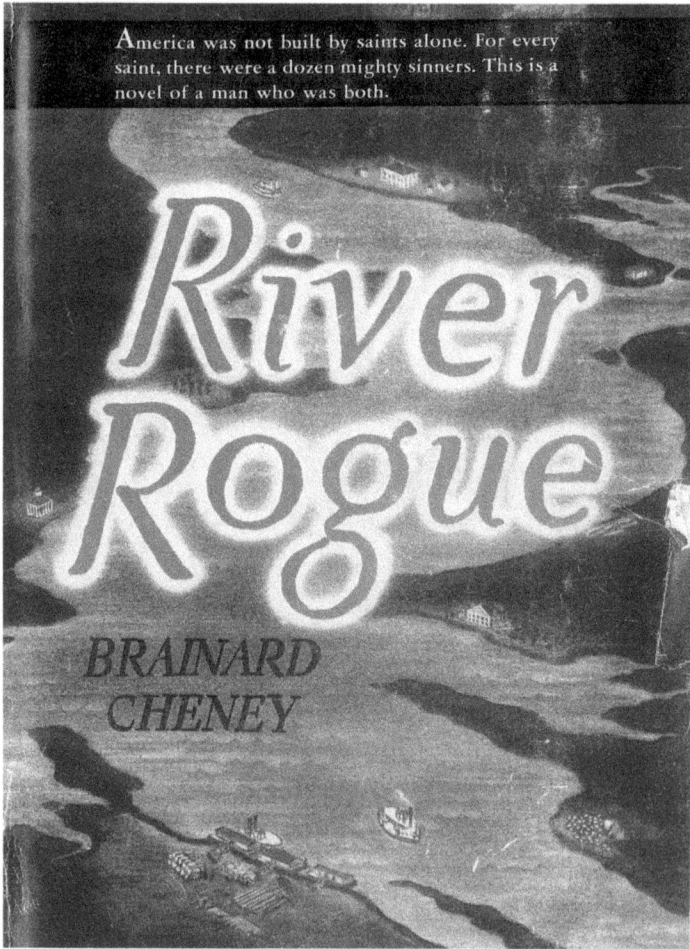

America was not built by saints alone. For every saint, there were a dozen mighty sinners. This is a novel of a man who was both.

River Rogue

BRAINARD CHENEY

Original cover for *River Rogue*, published in 1942

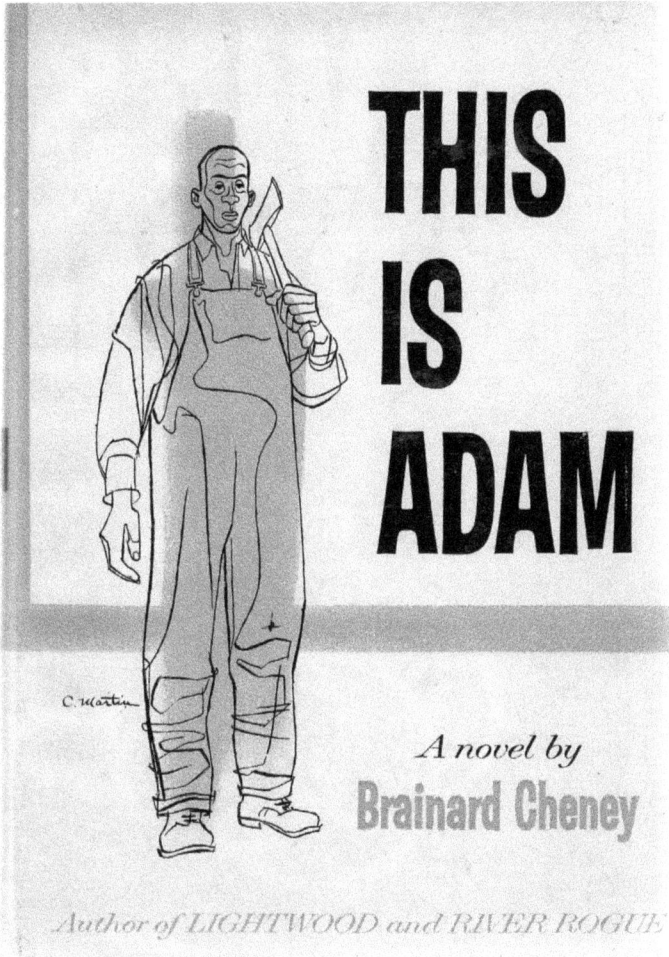

Original cover for *This is Adam*, published in 1958

Original cover for *Devil's Elbow*, published in 1969

Lucius Lazarus Williams, an ancestor of the author. Killed by Dodge Company agents in 1895, was character Jock Ruskin in *Lightwood*

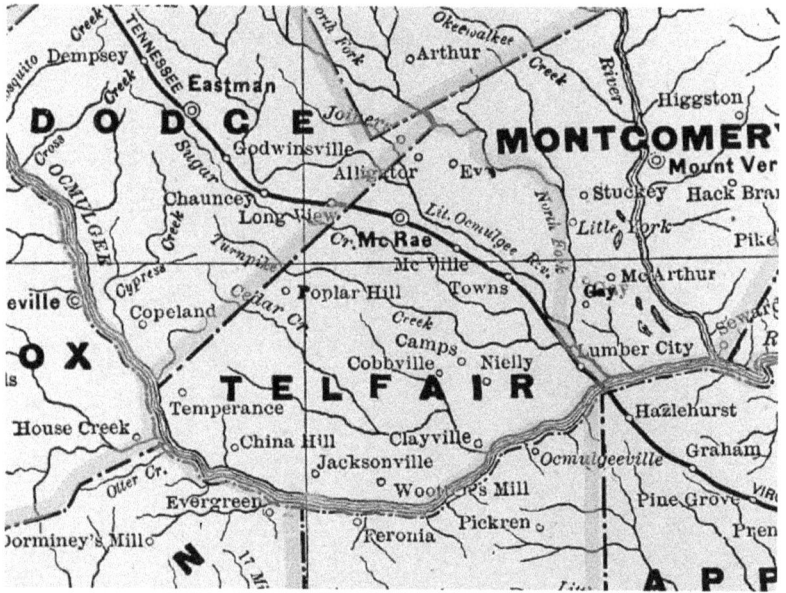

Detail from 1890 Georgia map showing Dodge and Telfair counties

4.

River Rogue: Unraveling the Past

Yeah, I know. Y'all kill stray house cats, usin' a shotgun—buckshot—a-pullin' both barrels. [...]. I stood theah and seen this half-a-peck of gall 'n' gizzard throw a twelve-foot 'gaitor. I mean crawl on top of 'im and stay theah [...].But after 'bout half 'n hour, heah 'e come swimmin' back with one hand. [...].I thought the gaitor had got the other un, but, hell naw, he 'uz a-holdin' the 'gaitor's eyeballs in it.

—Brainard Cheney, from his novel *River Rogue*

The critical tradition of Brainard Cheney's *River Rogue* is scant to non-existent. The book was reviewed well upon publication but quickly faded into obscurity and out of print. In 1982, a festival celebrating the timber rafting tradition of the Altamaha River inspired a limited second printing of *River*

Rogue with a new introduction by Robert Penn Warren, but for the most part the novel has been dismissed as local color or regionalism. Warren, though a professed admirer of Cheney's novels, avoids in-depth analysis in his introduction to the Project RAFT festival edition of the novel, which covers only three pages. Though he refers to the novel as "gripping," he contents himself with praising the "sense of local color speech" rather than the psychological depth.

Critics have long failed to notice the psychological depth and the odd sexual aspect of the novel. Ashley Brown calls the novel a "picaresque work" which it is in the sense that the novel details the sometimes amusing struggles of an outsider climbing the social ladder of a society by his wits alone.[126] It is also, however, a powerful work of psychological realism that fits neatly within the agrarian tradition. Unlike most picaresque works, the novel is rarely if ever satirical, and Cheney clearly does not intend for Ratliff Sutton to be an object of amusement and ridicule.

The story of Ratliff Sutton is a story of class conflict, cultural struggle, and the rejection of modern society for the naturalistic life of the raftsman. Ultimately, along with Ratliff's rise in Darien and his betrayal of China Swann, Bud True, and the rafts-men, the revealing of the circumstances of Ratliff's adolescent life drives the novel.

Ratliff is a runaway white child raised in the swamplands of the Oconee River by a black family. The opening pages offer no explanation of how Ratliff came to live with Poss and Uncle Mundy, his surrogate brother and father, respectively. The exact circumstances of Ratliff's prepubescent life and questions as to his and his siblings' paternity are not answered until the end of the novel.

Meeting the confluence of the Oconee and Ocmulgee rivers on the initial rafting trip with Poss reminds Ratliff of the first time he saw the rivers meet:

> He had been on the river four days then, coming from home, from Nine-and-a-Quarter. The name seemed unfamiliar to him now, but it had been home. He thought of his mother's pink-checkered apron and his older brother Bob, coming from their stave mill with sawdust on his eyelashes, and little Mona's snaggle teeth, and that red, bald head...His face squinted suddenly, as if in pain, and his mind veered off.[127]

Although this passage provides the reader with some information about Ratliff's early life, such as the fact that he is a runaway of sorts, and that memories of his childhood bring him pain, it also raises certain questions.

For example, why is this memory so painful for Ratliff? Who is his father? Why did he run away from home? And more specifically, whose "red, bald head" is he remembering? As the novel progresses, Ratliff's sexual insecurity reveals itself. The action of the novel manifests itself in the chronological sequence of Ratliff's rise from raft-hand to timber tycoon in Darien, his fall, and his subsequent return to Longpond. However, the mystery of the novel, or what modern critics would refer to as "hermeneutics," manifests itself almost entirely in raising or answering questions about Ratliff's infantile life.

One of the first answers to the initial hermeneutic questions arises simultaneously with the first overtly racial marker of Ratliff's inferiority. After successfully completing his first rafting voyage for profit with Poss, he is taken advantage of by the raftsman, Diggs McMillan. Diggs, in a successful effort to claim the boy's raft for his own, insinuates a carnal relationship between Ratliff and the black family with whom he lives: "And you are the white-trash, renegade boy that lives with 'im—lives theah in the swamp with niggers, in the house with niggers—in the bed with 'em, too, I reckon."[128]

Diggs calls Ratliff a "white nigger," stating "You kain't name yore pappy, naer yore mammy, and you're just the same as a nigger."[129] This incident exposes the racism inherent in the culture and the time period, while muddling Ratliff's sense of belonging and racial identity. While accepted on equal terms and indeed as an adopted son by Uncle Mundy, Ratliff finds that he is not accepted in Darien society, nor among the raftsmen on the river. He is figured as "other" and is labeled black. The incident severely wounds Ratliff as he recalls a different slur he received as a child back in the town of his birth, Nine-and-a-Quarter, traveling with his brother. Mace Rawlins initially drew Ratliff's attention to his mother's sexual infidelity, asking Ratliff in regards to his brother, "What's his last name? Looks like yore pa's lease done run out befoh this un come."[130] Ratliff vomits as he reflects on the steamboat ride home:

> Then he knew for a second time the feeling that his clothes had suddenly been jerked off him, exposing privates strange and red, like a scorpion's throat—not like those of other boys; that the suspicion about his mother he had not even admitted to himself was true, and the whole town was talking about it.[131]

This theme of exposure of the genitals suggests a malignant and unhealthy shame, a displacement of his mother's sexual guilt onto himself. He has been psychologically mutilated by his mother's status as "whore."At this point in the text, it becomes clear that Ratliff's shame over his mother's sexual transgressions motivated his flight from Nine-and-a-Quarter—a flight away from sexual shame and insecurity and into the care of Uncle Mundy and the realm of perceived ra-

cial inferiority. Ratliff eventually decides not to hide from outsiders, comparing it in his mind to a hen turkey only allowing
tiny spurred "young gobblers" to tread her. From now on, he
decides, he will go out "to tangle with the long-spurred gobblers."[132]

It is interesting that once again he figures his racial inferiority as sexual and in this case imagines himself a female turkey being treaded by a male gobbler! He soon finds that ac-
ceptance even by locals is hard to come by. When the local
Dickerson boys visit Uncle Mundy to discuss a deal over boil-
ing down sturgeon for their oil, Ratliff reflects that he hadn't
"seen any white people that close in months."[133] The
Dickersons refer to Ratliff as an "albino nigger."[134] The term
seems fitting for Ratliff who clearly identifies more closely
with black society than white at this point. The taunts from
the Dickersons sting him like whip lashes, and his awareness
of his own cultural inferiority becomes the driving force in his
ambition to rise in Darien and plays a large role in his betrayal of his friends and his subsequent fall. (The taunts that Ratliff receives probably recall similar taunts Cheney endured
from his habit of sleeping at the black caretaker Robin Bess's
home during his childhood.) Ratliff somewhat redeems himself in the eyes of the Dickersons, when, rather than lose a
sturgeon he had gaffed, he ties the rope around his waist and
nearly drowns himself attempting to snag the fish. They ad-
mire him for his tenacity, but Ratliff later recognizes the fool-

ishness of this action when he dreams of his own corpse, fish-white and bloated. This theme of drowning due to reckless-ness and lack of respect for the river and the natural world will continue to occur in this and Cheney's later novels.

The action of the novel concerns itself with class opposi-tion between Yankee industrialists and the rural inhabitants of the Wiregrass region in the post-Reconstruction era. The two groups are historically manifested in the Northern-owned timber companies of Darien, Georgia, and the raftsmen of the Ocmulgee, Oconee, and Altamaha River systems. Cheney, in his representation of the companies' manipulation of the set-tlers accurately portrays the historical battle between these two groups, while critiquing the same "arrogance and self-assurance" among Unionists that the Agrarians believed re-sulted in the exploitation of the South after the Civil War.[135] Cheney's novel is agrarian in that Ratliff's failure results from his abandonment of the rural life of the river for the industrial life of Darien.

Ratliff's feelings of inferiority are compounded by his irre-sponsible decision to raft the river during flood stage, result-ing in the death of his black friend, Poss. Cheney's portrayal of black characters is much stronger in this novel than in his previous one, and much of the initial wisdom in the novel de-rives from Uncle Mundy and Poss, who warn him against the rafting trip. Poss cautions that it's a "rough ole river, lak dis" and Uncle Mundy admonishes: "You talk lak you ain't got much respeck for dis river, not like no raftsman."[136] Here we see the agrarian ideal personified in the black characters.

Religion plays almost no role in this early novel which predates Cheney's own religious conversion, but the natural world and specifically the river substitutes for the presence of God. Ratliff's lack of respect for the river and the memories of his early life on the Ocmulgee, which he refers to as a "God-damn son-of-a-bitch," precipitate his friend's death. Here one may easily witness the manner in which Cheney parallels the action of the novel with revelation. The dramatic scene of Poss's death is immediately preceded by a chain in the hermeneutic sequence, exposing more details about Ratliff's adolescent life. Ratliff, after noticing that he no longer can spot the shoreline through the foggy mist, is reminded of a sexually ambiguous scene from his early childhood in which he startled his mother and the local doctor by opening the door to her bedroom: "The faces brought him a feeling of confused suspicion. They were standing at her bedroom door, where they had started up from their seats as he opened it. What the hell! What the hell! he thought."[137]

Immediately after this enigmatic sequence, a steamboat appears out of the early morning mist, forcing them to crash the raft into the bank. The river drowns Poss, closing the first section of the novel. In his "I See Sunday" essay published later in his career, Cheney states that the river contributes "controlling action" to the novel. It "becomes a moral force and a mythopoeic stimulus."[138] This "controlling action" quality of the river is present in this scene more so than anywhere else in the novel. The river, though often the scene of Ratliff's greatest triumphs and near superhuman ability at times, as evidenced by the picaresque scene in which he brutally wrestles an alligator, gouging its eyes out, is also quick and severe in its punishment for rash judgment and lack of respect. Everyone in the novel recognizes Ratliff's responsibility in Poss's death and this sense of guilt, alongside the racial and sexual guilt that Ratliff assumes, becomes a major factor in the development of Ratliff's insecurity.

Part Two of the novel begins with Ratliff returning to the river after a long hiatus to drift timber with Bud True, a legendary raftsman. Early in the trip, the storeowner Grizzard deals Ratliff another harsh blow as Ratliff realizes several miles downriver that the man has cheated him out of his potatoes and sold him rancid meat. After tying up the raft and walking back upriver to the store, Bud True, while rubbing a piece of the maggoty salt pork in Grizzard's face, articulates the motivation behind Grizzard's crime:

> "Thought you put off rotten meat on this boy,
> kaze he tore up a raft and drowned a man, eh?
> Treat 'im like a dog—no, a hog—no, by God,
> yuh wouldn't feed such meat to yo' hogs!"[139]

Here in the novel, True solidifies Ratliff's early loyalty to him as well as his determination not to make foolhardy mistakes in the future. Gleeful after punishing the storeowner, Ratliff suggests that the men get drunk to celebrate. True responds with the warning, "Don't you start hintin' at quittin' a raft you done turned loose on the river with!" Ratliff answers, " 'Sho', Mister Bud. I hadn't seen it that way."[140]

Poss's death has a severe, but temporary effect on Ratliff's sexual activity in that he associates his sexual shame with his carelessness in drowning Poss. A local brothel owner, China Swann, has attempted to take Ratliff for a lover, and he relates the events to one another: "He couldn't make himself feel right about being there: somehow China was tied up in the hell-bending that had sent him out onto the river on the freshet to drown Poss."[141] Bud recognizes Ratliff's sexual insecurities, referring to the boy as "skirt-scared."[142] This initial lack of sexual activity differentiates him from the other raftsmen, legendary hell raisers and frequenters of brothels both historically and in Cheney's novel. Ratliff eventually does become sexually active, but a certain shame follows him throughout the novel, most visible in the problems with Captain Seborn Henry, China's first lover. Again, we see parallels with Cheney's own life as the drowning of his friend Robert Willcox affected his own sexual ability for years after the event, as described in *Devil's Elbow* and Cheney's "I See Sunday" essay.

The sexual conflict in *River Rogue* parallels the central opposition: the dichotomy of the raftsmen and the Yankee-owned timber companies. The raftsmen complain that the companies engage in price fixing and illegal or unfair measurement or grading standards. The river only flows one way, and raftsmen must sell their logs at whatever price is available when they get to Darien or else pay costly storage fees, waiting for the price to go back up. Ratliff's opposition to the timber companies climaxes when one of their inspectors finds an illegal plug in his raft, subsequently banning him from the river and rafting. Ratliff takes to the backwoods and alluvial plains of the rivers, perfecting his method of plugging knots and scars in the logs and teaching it to any farmer willing to learn.

Ratliff sums up the conflict between the raftsmen and the companies in his words at Mosquito Bight:

> It ain't even a gamble. The damn companies stack the cards and cut 'em both. They keep the deal all the time, and if you put into theah place you've got to play theah game. The only card you ever could slip in was log-doctorin', and it waun't much, but now they're tryin' to put yuh on the chain gang for that.[143]

This passage represents the general attitude of the raftsmen toward the companies. Ratliff feels that the companies are manipulating him and the other raftsmen out of their timber by methods that he does not understand. His only recourse is to utilize methods familiar to him and his culture to combat the companies—log doctoring.

Ratliff's success at log plugging prompts the Pitt timber company to offer him a job as timber inspector—that is a person whose job it is to find doctored logs such as the ones that Ratliff has been selling to the company. As Ratliff mulls over whether to take the job, the image of the raftsmen he would betray with his action rises before him: "Beyond the road, beyond the rim of his vision, were vague gray forms, watching raftsmen—he did not look at them, but he knew they were there, knew their faces. [...] the gray forms clung to the rim of his consciousness."[144] The ghosts of the raftsmen cement his decision not to work for the company. In a clever and amusing form of revenge, Ratliff convinces Marmaduke Pitt of his willingness to work as inspector as he manipulates the company into dropping the legal charges against him, while selling them a raft full of hollow logs.

Ratliff's next action is a failed revolution precipitated by the Panic of 1893. After finding that the price of timber has again been cut by the companies, he attempts to rally the men into aggressive opposition by forming a boom of rafts across the river above Darien, thereby stopping the flow of timber into the town and starving the market.

Ratliff, in one of the most fantastic scenes of the novel, pushes his raft away from the public boom at Darien, and riding on the force of the rising tide, actually floats the raft 20 miles upstream to Clayhole Creek with the other raftsmen behind him. His failure to convince them that night to unite in opposition to the companies results in his utter disillusionment with their cause and his abandonment of life on the river. It is reminiscent in many respects of Micajah's Corn's disillusionment with the Squatters cause after he fails to rally the alliance men to burn the company mill and kill Zenas Fears in *Lightwood*. In both novels, the initial rejection of a plot against the company by the squatters/raftsmen precipitates the fall of the main character, who is left feeling betrayed.

Ratliff negates his former life as a raftsman, attempting to break into the strata of society in the town through the purchase of two taverns, the second of which requires a loan from China Swann, his brothel-keeping mistress. He quickly befriends Geoffrey Dale, the son of the owner of the largest company in Darien. As Ratliff attempts to achieve higher status in Darien, he is forced to compromise his origins, both altering his manner of speech and his habits, reflecting that "Darien would accept no outsider as a public inspector."[145] Oxford educated and the son of an Englishman only 30 years in America, Dale is the antithesis of Ratliff, the orphan raised by blacks along the sallow banks of the Oconee River. They become unlikely friends as Geoffrey helps Ratliff to break into the upper social circles of Darien, their friendship ending in tragedy and death as a result of Ratliff's marriage to Geoffrey's cousin Robbie.

After meeting with initial failure in his bid to gain a job as public timber inspector, Ratliff asks China to leave Darien for the Oconee with him. She refuses, expressing in bitter terms the reasons to stay in Darien:

> You're tryin' to take the easy way out, to crawfish. You knew Darien was a son-of-a-bitch when you come here, but you aimed to make her your son-of-a-bitch. You swore to quittin' the river for good—to quit sweatin', stealin', freezin', fightin' over logs to make Darienites rich—raftsmen were born suckers, and you quit 'em to work your way into the big money, take your share from the smart men.[146]

China manipulates Ratliff into staying in Darien by playing on his sensibilities. She belittles the life of a raftsman and dramatizes the conflict as a choice between the "born suckers" (raftsmen) and the "smart men" (Darienites).

Ratliff eventually acquires the job of public timber scaler, and works his way into the "big money," but, in doing so, he is forced to abandon China Swann and Bud True for Robbie MacGregor and Geoffrey Dale. Ratliff's role as timber inspector pits him on the side of the companies, thereby betraying his former friends, the raftsmen.

Ratliff's success in marrying Robbie and rising to social prominence in Darien entails an inherent abandonment of what Robert Penn Warren refers to as the "old world" of the novel.[147] His elopement with the girl does not, moreover, have the reaction he expects, as Robbie's father dies and Geoffrey Dale and Darien society turns against him. After losing both Robbie's father and his job as timber inspector, Ratliff, in a scene reminiscent of Lear, rides into a storm, only to fall off of his horse and witness a hurricane of mammoth proportions destroy the timber boom at Darien, scattering the logs into the sea. As in *Lightwood*, here we see Cheney's marvelous ability to weave fact and fiction into his novels. The hurricane of October 3, 1898 and the resulting destruction of the timber boom is a very real incident in the history of Darien, Georgia. The *Darien Gazette* estimated that between 40 to 50 people lost their lives, reporting that hundreds of men were required to recover the lost timber and that crews were at work for months.[148]

This incident becomes the major factor in Ratliff's perceived salvation. His genius as a timberman affords ample opportunity after the chaos of the storm. As every company in Darien races to retrieve their logs amid the chaos, Ratliff secures every log he can get his hands on, regardless of the true owner, hiding the timber far upriver within the confines of a hidden oxbow lake. Later, he brings a portable sawmill to the lake, thereby starting his own timber firm, just at the moment when the other firms of Darien are faltering due to the incredible losses they suffered from the storm. Ratliff's greatest betrayal of his friends comes during the course of this action. He enlists the help of the former raftsmen to carry out this venture, cheating them out of the bulk of the profits and obscuring his real motivation in starting the firm: greed and a twisted sense of revenge against the companies. Here he begins to take on characteristics of another main character in Cheney's novels, Calhoun Calebb from *Lightwood*.

Bud True and China come to recognize Ratliff's betrayal. These two characters differ from Ratliff in that they maintain their integrity throughout the novel. Such a statement might seem ill-considered in the face of the fact that Bud True murders Ratliff's innocent wife, Robbie, in a drunken rage, but the point is that Bud *True* remains *true* to both himself and Ratliff. He recognizes the point at which Ratliff's ambition in his rise has surpassed his motivation to benefit the raftsmen at the companies' expense. Bud True describes Ratliff's disloyalty in bitter terms:

> You done son-of-a-bitched me—all your
> friends, gittin' ready to, them you ain't al-

ready. I know what you aim to do, done heard: quick as you weed out some of these heah companies, get holt o' the thing, you aim to take all us ragged assed rafthands timber for nuthin'—give us ration money—weevily ration money.[149]

Even when confronted by Ratliff after his murder of Robbie, True does not fall back on his drunkenness and blind despair as an excuse: "'I done it, Snake, and I'm man enough to take the consequences. 'Tain't nuthin' to be gained a-mouthin' 'bout it!"[150]

China has a similar take on Ratliff's betrayal: "The son-of-a-bitch *did* me all right!" She later reflects that she is partly responsible for Ratliff's behavior by making him abandon his life as a raftsman: "She should never have talked Snake into coming to Darien in the first place—it was part her fault."[151] The action of the novel, is, at this point, yet to be resolved. The questions raised at the beginning of the novel, are here answered, however, shedding a great deal of light on Ratliff's choice in women, and partly assuming responsibility for the tragedy in his life.

Throughout the novel, Ratliff's relationship with China is punctuated by the recurring appearance of the steamboat captain, Seborn Henry. Ratliff's initial reservations about making love to China are precipitated by her relationship with this man whom Ratliff seems to hold in high regard. Ratliff reflects that Henry helped Ratliff's family after his father's death. Even after accepting China as a lover, however, Ratliff continues to demonstrate occasional reluctance to go to bed with her. At one point he tells China, "I don't pay a debt by foulin' a fellow's bed—even if he is fool enough to keep a woman like you in it!" China notes as Ratliff's leaves the curious look on Ratliff's face "like there *was* something between him and Seborn and he didn't want to talk about it."[152] Soon after, Seborn Henry further complicates this already enigmatic relationship by attempting to crash Ratliff's raft with his steamboat. After Ratliff's betrayal of China, she, Bud, and Henry meet for drinks at the Birdcage, her whorehouse. Here Henry reveals that he is the father of Ratliff's bastard brother—that it was he in fact who Ratliff's mother took as a lover prematurely, after Ratliff's father's death.

Although Cheney presents this revelation to the reader and not Ratliff, one can be certain that Ratliff has been aware of Henry's relationship with his mother all along, at least on some level. This situation becomes even more interesting as it occurs quick on the heels of Ratliff's identification of his wife Robbie with his mother. Kneeling at her bedside, in a state of mental turmoil, begging for their reconciliation, Ratliff is reminded of his childhood:

It was the first time that he had sat on a has-
sock, sat at a woman's knees, since he was a
little boy, and he was dumb—his stomach
burned and quivered and he could not control
the shaking of his shoulders. Then he found
that he was talking—not knowing what he said
or why. His ugliness, his cruelty came of hard
licks, beginning here—his own mother—when
he was a boy. She had betrayed him, after his
father's death, with another man—had borne a
bastard child.[153]

Ratliff clearly identifies the kneeling posture he has taken
at Robbie's bedside with a similar humble position he once
took in front of his mother. Robbie becomes a mother figure
for him in the novel and the threat of losing her love echoes
Ratliff's earlier loss of his mother.

Cheney emphasizes the importance of this reading of the
novel for himself in his essay, " 'Look-a, Look-a Yonder—I See
Sunday, I See Sunday!' Or, a Deliverer Delivered," stating
that, rereading the novel he found that he had "fumbled Sutton's ill-fated romance with Robbie, daughter of the Darien
uppercrust, in the next to last chapter. I failed to get out of my
head and onto the page his Garden of Eden image of his
mother that was what he really saw in Robbie, was really in
love with."[154] Ratliff has been searching for his mother not

only in Robbie but also in China, the woman who shares with his mother a lover, Captain Seborn Henry. For Ratliff, his mother is both virgin and whore, symbolized in Robbie and China, respectively. The resolution of these issues is predicated by the inevitable and tragic conclusion of the action in the following scenes, the results of Ratliff's Oedipal desire and his betrayal of his friends.

Robert Penn Warren calls Bud True's murder of Robbie "a stroke of fate" and "a blow against Sutton for deserting the old world."[155] In that sense, it is comparable to Micajah Corn's paralysis in *Lightwood*. Both events precipitate the final tragedy in the respective novels. In Penn Warren's words, "True's failure and despair overcome him, and blindly he strikes Robbie down with his crutch."[156] Bud can no longer abide Ratliff's perceived mistreatment of him."Friend!" he exclaims, "Not since you quit the river, not."[157] Bud's murder of Robbie, brought on by her reproaching him for his failure to acquire treatment for his sick wife, tragically brings the story to a close. Ratliff recognizes that he is ultimately to blame as well as Bud and that no redemption will be afforded him in Darien.

After visiting Bud True in jail, Ratliff faces brutal shame in the realization of his betrayal. Ratliff refuses to testify against Bud True. He seeks redemption with the final words of the novel:

'It is this,' he said: 'I think the defendant, Bud True, is plainly insane and was insane when he killed my wife. I will not agree to prosecute him.' He turned, putting his black hat on his head, and spoke to McDeeds as he passed him. 'You can reach me in the future at Longpond: I'll be up on the Oconee.' He walked out of the room, from the courthouse and into the sunlight.[158]

With these words, Ratliff offers Bud True a fair shot at freedom and rightfully assumes an appropriate amount of guilt for himself over his wife's death.

Robert Penn Warren writes that Ratliff is "going back to the Oconee to find something he has lost," but Warren hesitates to state what that "something" is.[159] In leaving Darien, Ratliff rejects not only the realities of habitation in that specific city, but all of modern society, while embracing the possibilities of life in a more rural, more naturalistic environment. Ratliff is most at home on the river.

Cheney's best writing glows with his remarkable description of the Altamaha flood plain. Earlier in the novel, Ratliff fled China's brothel and returned to the river for a fishing trip, glad "the smell of Darien and the Birdcage was out of his nose."[160] The springtime river is rife with fertility and beauty:

It was spring, just turning summer, and everything that could was blooming, looked like.
The willow piles had turned from gold to
green, May haws and crabapples were dusting
the ground around them, like a miller's apron,
and wide-open bay blossoms were shedding
their matches. In the pockets and ponds, yellow and white and blue water lilies spotted the
pads, and in the low swamp there were fields
of flags. The redbirds and kingfishers kept a
bright flicker moving up and down the river
bank, and the white cranes and curlew in the
sun were so bright it hurt your eye to look at
them."[161]

The introduction to *I'll Take My Stand* states: "We receive
the illusion of having power over nature, and lose the sense of
nature as something mysterious and contingent."[162] Mark
Malvasi characterizes this mindset in the following way, "The
essence of Agrarian thought lies in its persuasive challenge to
the assumption that heaven can be made immanent, can be
established on earth."[163]

Ratliff "Snake" Suttons' failure rests on that assumption,
and his only recourse after leaving the courthouse is to attempt to establish a purer, more enduring style of life on the
banks of the oxbow lake, Longpond.

Notes

[126] Brown, 60.

[127] Cheney, *River Rogue*, 15.

[128] Ibid,22.

[129] Ibid.

[130] Ibid, 25.

[131] Ibid.

[132] Ibid, 31.

[133] Ibid.

[134] Ibid, 35.

[135] Malvasi, 14.

[136] Cheney, *River Rogue*, 118.

[137] Ibid, 123.

[138] Cheney, "I See Sunday," 160.

[139] Cheney, *River Rogue*, 137.

[140] Ibid, 139.

[141] Ibid, 143.

[142] Ibid, 144.

[143] Ibid, 253.

[144] Ibid, 264.

[145] Ibid, 334.

[146] Ibid, 319-20.

[147] Warren, Robert Penn. "Introduction." *River Rogue*. Washington, DC: Burr Oak Publishers, 1982, 3.

[148] Sullivan, Buddy. *Early Days on the Georgia Tidewater: the Story of McIntosh County and Sapelo.* Darien: Darien News, 1990.

[149] Cheney, *River Rogue*, 412.

[150] Ibid, 446.

[151] Ibid, 428, 431.

[152] Ibid, 191.

[153] Ibid, 417-18.

[154] Cheney, "I See Sunday," 166.

[155] Warren, Introduction, 3.

[156] Ibid.

[157] Cheney, *River Rogue*, 446.

[158] Ibid, 452.

[159] Warren, Introduction, 3.

[160] Cheney, *River Rogue*, 177.

[161] Ibid.

[162] Rubin, xxiv.

[163] Malvasi, 21.

·

5.

This is Adam: Race and Religious Conversion

> The view grew misty and a current rose up
> through him, as if from the ground. A current
> from the old field itself—their experience to-
> gether—of hunger and fulfillment, of high wa-
> ter and waiting, of sweat and strain and anx-
> iousness, but at last the warming sight of a
> snowstorm of open cotton bolls. Till now. He
> turned his back on the field and wiped his eyes
> with his hand.

—Brainard Cheney, from his novel *This is Adam*

This is Adam is the only one of Cheney's novels to centrally
address racial issues in the post-Reconstruction South. If
Lightwood and *River Rogue* are about the death of the agrarian vision, then this novel is about what happens to those of
honor and spirit who remain after that vision dies, specifically

in the character, Adam Atwell. Once again Cheney critiques the manner in which unfettered capitalism and economic depravity have come to destroy the agrarian way of life that once existed along the Oconee River.

In what Ashley Brown describes as "probably Cheney's best novel," Cheney presents the white men of the town, albeit business leaders or simple landowners whose land interests coincide with that of the Hightowers, as motivated by industrialization, greed, and money.[164] They are villains, while Adam Atwell himself, representative of African-American sharecroppers of the time period, is virtuous and simple, yet endowed with keen insight into the character of others.

This is Adam details the circumstances of a large land deal in the town of Riverton, modeled on Cheney's boyhood home of Lumber City, Georgia, which lies near the confluence of the Ocmulgee and Oconee rivers. Lucy Hightower, a widow, attempts to sell her estate to a northern developer to move her family to Charleston and raise her children in a more civilized environment. Her Charleston upbringing has caused her to regard Riverton as a wicked community.

Forced to rely on unscrupulous local profiteers such as the banker Littleton, the widow Hightower looks to the African-American overseer Adam as the only bastion of integrity and honesty to which she can turn. Intensely autobiographical, Cheney's novel addresses the conflict between the widow's intent regarding her children and the loss of the family estate, most deeply felt by Adam. Cheney dedicates the novel to Robin Bess, his mother's own African-American overseer and the basis for Adam Atwell in the novel. Cheney's mother was from the prominent Mood family of Charleston and is represented here as Lucy Hightower. The deceased Colonel Hightower is obviously Cheney's father, Colonel Brainard B. Cheney, while the young Marcellus Hightower embodies Cheney himself.

Cheney's handling of race in his novels improved as he grew as a writer and a person. The black characters in *Lightwood* are rarely complex and are generally presented alongside the company as existential threats to the white characters' way of life. One of the most vivid scenes of *Lightwood*, the Lancaster race riot, is also the most questionable from a racial perspective. Essentially, Cheney describes a black horde descending on the town and threatening the white citizens. Cheney depicts the leaders of the mob shouting: "Kill any white man, but don't kill Yankee."[165] The irony is rooted in the fact that the blacks wind up killing a Yankee, and an innocent one at that.

This is Adam notably presents the same incident but this time from the perspective of a black man, falsely tried and imprisoned for the crime. The novel makes it clear that in the aftermath of the riot, white officials simply seized as many blacks as they could lay hands on and tried them all regardless of guilt or innocence. Adam notes that none of them claimed to have been actually involved in the killing. They were all found guilty, nevertheless, and sentenced to life at the Lost Mountain Prison, a deplorable coal mining operation. The contrast in tone between Cheney's two fictional portrayals of this historic event is striking and reflects Cheney's own changing views on race and the Civil Rights movement, which was in full swing by the time of *This is Adam*'s publication in 1958.

Cheney's first novel does pay some attention to racial issues, often exposing deliberate cruelty by whites against blacks. The fact that the villain of the novel rides a horse (a black stallion) named "Nigger" shocks a modern reader but seems to be an intentional effort to expose Calhoun Calebb's insensitivity, as does the McIntosh family's referral to the deaf mute, Uncle Tom-type servant in the family as "Dummy."

In *Lightwood*, the Lancaster trial of the accused rioters is quite distasteful to a modern reader. There is little doubt that Cheney intended that it be so; still he plays some of the events for laughs, and he cannot help but to point out the "body smell of negroes" that hung in the humid air of the courtroom.[166] This kind of language is turned on its head in *This is Adam* where Adam frequently reflects on the alien smell of white men, which he describes as "anathema" in his nostrils. Cheney clearly had in mind some of the racially dated language from his earlier novel when he wrote *This is Adam*.

One of the most racially problematic parts of *Lightwood* would be the character of King Charles, whom Cheney uses alternately for comic and dramatic effect. His character confirms many of the worst stereotypes regarding blacks. Zeke decides to bring King Charles along on a trip to sabotage a Coventry raft train floating down the Altamaha to Darien. Cheney describes Charles in racially stereotypical terms, characteristic of the time period. He is a "blue-black, thick, square-cut negro whose nostrils and lips flared out like the edge of a turtle's shell."[167] Micajah is rightly reticent around Charles, recognizing the dangers of bringing him into their trust. He is filled with irritation, and later in private rails against Zeke for bringing "that loud-mouthed nigger down here."[168]

Cheney describes King Charles as ominous several times and then has him relate a deprecatory and exaggerated story about Littleton to Micajah. The story is about the time when the two of them headed to Darien on a pickup raft of just seven logs and Littleton committed several reckless acts. At one time, they bluffed a group of men with guns into letting them claim some logs floating along a riverbank. Later, they nearly broke up the raft by snagging a log on the bank while running full speed down the river. They gambled away all of the money from the sale so that Littleton and King Charles had to walk the 150 miles back home. Cheney plays the story for laughs but also to demonstrate again the loose-talking manner and untrustworthiness of King Charles. The problem of Charles is solved for Micajah when the tie rope accidentally slides around his finger and rips it off as Micajah takes off in the raft. The tone here smacks of minstrelsy as King Charles "let out a gunshot blast from his backside" when his finger was severed. The scatological humor here seems out of place and solely to provoke amusement at the figure who earlier seemed so ominous.

All of Micajah's fears about him are confirmed when Kathleen McIntosh encounters King Charles, and he divulges details about the Corns' raft sabotaging to her, the daughter of Captain McIntosh, who works for the company. On Zeke and Littleton's next trip, Zenas Fears lies in wait for them in a pup tent on the raft. He kills Zeke and sends his body to the bottom of the Ocmulgee. Cheney implies that Zeke's death was caused, in part, by the loose talk from the foolish King Charles. The novel suggests that perhaps Kathleen had told her father what she had learned from King Charles, leading to the ambush. Interestingly, Cheney includes the King Charles story again in *This is Adam*, told in a different form. In this case, the story is related second hand by Marcellus to his mother, and the story serves primarily to emphasize the treachery and foolishness of a white man in the novel, Peter Bright, and Adam's suffering at his hand. Again, a reader feels that Cheney was compensating for his earlier novel's lack of racial sensitivity when he was writing his later novels.

In *River Rogue* the main character identifies racially as black at least at the beginning of the novel, which features at least two strong black characters, Poss and Uncle Mundy. Both are endowed with wisdom, and both are modeled at least somewhat on Robin Bess, but once again the wisdom features as foreign and alien to the main character. Ratliff does not respect Uncle Mundy's witch doctoring and other advice, often at his peril.

The complexity of the black characters in this novel probably derives from Cheney's consultations with Robin Bess while working on the book. The psychological taunting that Ratliff endures for living with blacks echoes the taunting that the young Cheney received in Lumber City because of his close relationship with Robin Bess, who sometimes served as a surrogate father. Still, in *River Rogue*, Poss is a sidekick at best. He and Uncle Mundy die relatively early in the novel before we truly see them fleshed out as characters.

With *This is Adam*, we see Cheney dealing overtly with issues of race for the first time. The novel is clearly a product of the dawning Civil Rights era and reflects Cheney's changing views on race. His initial title for the novel was supposed to have been *I Bent My Back to the Oppressor*, which demonstrates that it was conceived as an indictment of white oppression of African Americans all along. The title refers to the metaphorical bending of Adam's back in labor to whites. However, it seems that Cheney intends a literal meaning as well since the novel continually features Adam stooping at the steps of the Hightower home in his conversations with Mrs.

Hightower. Despite the fact that she treats him more justly than any of the other white characters in the novel, with the exception of her son Marcellus, she is still his oppressor in several senses of the word. Cheney was definitely aware of this, as indicated in a letter to Flannery O'Connor where he stated that he planned to "use the ritual at the steps between Lucy Hightower and Adam Atwell as a rhythm of sorts throughout the book, ending with it, I hope, for a total significance."[169]

The writing of this novel coincided with the end of Cheney's political affiliation with Governor Frank Clement of Tennessee over the matter of segregation. In a letter to Flannery O'Connor, Cheney claims to be unable to "stomach" Clement's candidate for governor, Buford Ellington, who "made a backhanded invitation to the Ku Klux Klan, et al. to the effect that he would close down any school at their behest before they would let it be desegregated."[170] Cheney describes Ellington as a "Mississippi redneck" and states that he does not aim "to be a party to the rise of Mississippi redneck-ism in Tennessee!"[171] Ironically, Cheney got his own taste of racial prejudice when the *Atlanta Journal Constitution* refused to review *This is Adam* because "it was about niggers."[172] Flannery O'Connor reported this to Cheney who checked it out for himself and found it was accurate. In fact, the book editor at the Constitution thought that Cheney himself "was a negro. But said he wouldn't review it anyhow because it was about negroes."[173]

Cheney ultimately talked to Ralph McGill, an old friend and the chief editor of the newspaper, who arranged for the novel to be reviewed.

In the novel, Adam is a mulatto black man, sired by a white slave owner. Adam found himself indebted to Colonel Hightower, who successfully freed him from the Lost Mountain prison after Adam was unjustly convicted in the murder of a white man in the Lancaster riot. Now, two years after the death of the Colonel, Adam exists in a relationship of mutual dependence with the widow Hightower.

Through Adam's point of view, the novel eulogizes an earlier, more honorable time, when the late Colonel Hightower was alive. Integrity was still to be found among the yeoman farmers of the Wiregrass region during this earlier period, before economic depravity and the inevitable decline of an age led to corruption, hardship, and villainy. The novel warns of the tragedy inherent in the Land Deal, a prostitution of the archaic agrarian vision personified in Adam Atwell. Economic necessity, compounded by the death of Colonel Hightower, and her recognition of the evil inherent in the people of Riverton, pressures Mrs. Hightower to forsake her land holdings and son's inheritance for the luxury of Charleston and the love of her childhood sweetheart, Edward Louthan.

Cheney presents Adam in a much more favorable light than any of the white characters in the novel. Adam, within the modern world of Riverton, is an anachronism. He has yet to forsake the agrarian lifestyle and still believes in the virtues of the natural world and his archaic way of life.

The Riverton Bank symbolizes both the manner in which white profiteers manipulate Adam, as well as the way in which the industrialized world often oppresses those possessing traditional values. Adam is not comfortable within the bank in Riverton and regards the banker, Littleton, as an unscrupulous and conniving man, but a man to whom respect must be paid within the social and economic confines of the era and region. Upon entering the bank Adam feels "as he always did, a little dazzled and trying to get his bearings."[174] The atmosphere is "high and rarefied," at odds with the simple cabin with kerosene lighting in which Adam makes his home.[175]

The banker Littleton exerts superiority over Adam by questioning why Adam is taking out such a large sum of money. He calls into question Adam's credibility as a bank customer and his ability to administer his own finances. Adam recalls an incident from four years past in which Littleton refused to let Adam count his cash at the window and then refused to correct an error, only to discover that the error was in Adam's favor. Cheney reveals the tremendous gap in the integrity of the two men within this scene. Adam actually saves Littleton twenty dollars by pointing out the mistake. The scene emphasizes Adam's simple honesty, while demonstrating the unfettered greed of Littleton, eager to take advantage at every step. Adam's insight into the motivations of Littleton as well as the other characters who play a role in the Land Deal reveals him to be a man of keen intelligence.

Within Adam's world view and the novel's, Littleton is not to blame so much as the entire profession of banking and possibly the social construction of a society based on greed and racism. Adam recognizes that: "A banker was always out to hook you for something if he could (especially if your skin was black) but you had to live with him."[176]

Cheney further emphasizes Adam's resistance to the modern world in his aversion to the electricity in a lawyers' office. Later in the story, he feels that the lawyers are "trying to push that electric lamp onto him," and he associates the white lawyers with the white faces of the jury who convicted him after the Lancaster race riot: *The thing was that those white people had denied him a human skin. And that was what he had seen again on the white men's faces in lawyer Duke's office.*[177]

The introduction into the novel of the Lancaster race riot makes an interesting connection with Cheney's first novel, *Lightwood*, and constitutes an overt treatment of the historical incident. Interestingly, while in *Lightwood* one witnessed the incident through the eyes of the white victim of the mob, his family, and the prosecuting attorney in the trial, in *This is Adam* the reader is afforded the opportunity to view the act through the eyes of an innocent black man tried for the crime, Adam Atwell. Adam, having the misfortune to pass out in a barn and sleep through the entire incident, awakes only to be arrested for the crime, along with several others. Sentenced to hard labor in the mines, he is eventually freed by the defending attorney in the trial, Colonel Hightower. Colonel Hightower, although the novel begins after his death, represents the ideal of the early agrarian spirit, a successful farmer, one of the few white characters in the novel at all sympathetic to the plight of African-Americans.

The novel soon informs the reader of the high regard that Adam held for the late Colonel Hightower. He derived his insight and world view from the Colonel. On his deathbed, the Colonel informs Adam that "There are things that count more than money, Adam. There are things worse than not having enough to wear and to eat—and I've known want...when you come to die...I know now that where I made my mistake was in not taking *it* into my calculations."[178]

Adam ponders over the Colonel's meaning: "*Calculations! What was it that the Colonel had been talking about?*"[179] The meaning of the Colonel's statement overtly refers to his own unexpected death as well as the treachery of his understudy, Oswald Paley. The "it" to which the dying Colonel refers, however, is also the intangible encroachment of industrialization, a coming rape of the land, and the corruption of a people that follows such an encroachment. Adam well heeds this knowledge of the Colonel's and uses it as a guide for his life. He recognizes that he will one day be freed from his bondage to the land, as a poor sharecropper. The Colonel had promised him the Wyche field and Adam had once possessed constant faith in this promise and in the field itself. Adam reflects on the Colonel's dying words after he learns of the widow's coming land deal. He tells his mother that "She goin' ter sell the swamp."[180] His mother asks, "Wyche field, too?" The novel demonstrates the strong ties that Adam has to this piece of land in his reaction:

> There was a sudden chill on the air, coming from where his mother stood like a dark foreboding shadow. Adam shuddered and repeated, "Wyche field, too." But, as the words came off his tongue, the yellow mud plot of cleared river swamp seemed to him a tenuous, a chancy, and slight assurance to the future.[181]

Adam clearly holds the Wyche field in the highest regard. It is the finest piece of farmland he has ever known. He relies on it each year for his sustenance, and he takes pride and joy in its tending and care. The river runs close to the field and floods it nearly every spring, the floodwaters acting as a natural fertilizer, allowing Adam to plant his crop only after the water subsides:

Ordinarily, it didn't get dry enough to plow the swamp field till later than this. He had planted cotton there as late as June and made a crop! His face began to glow, and he lifted his arm and the hat, like the soaring wing of an eagle. Yessir, he had had catfish gnaw his corn off the cobs in the old Wyche field and then replanted and made a crop. He smiled with an absorption oblivious of the point he had set out to prove. But then, to be sure, there was not another piece of ground in this end of the county like the Wyche field![182]

Adam's preoccupation with the virtues of the Wyche field recalls Micajah Corn's love of and reliance upon the Sugar Field in *Lightwood.* Both of these landmarks serve as symbols of agrarian life in their fertility and symbiotic relationship with Adam Atwell and Micajah Corn. This theme runs stronger in *This is Adam,* a novel in which the field is located within the river flood plain, and is cyclically flooded and fertilized by the spring freshets each year. Through his connection with the Wyche field, Adam establishes a symbiotic relationship with the river itself and its flood stages. Adam often reaches epiphanies when gazing at nature, actively searching out the Wyche field to do much of his thinking. This relationship reaches a climax when the dream of the river saves Adam's life at the end of the novel.

Cheney's novels fit comfortably together not just thematically, but along a geographic and temporal continuum as well. Lucy Hightower, reminiscing on the past, remembers she and Colonel Hightower's early days in Lancaster, recalling characters, events, and locations from *Lightwood* and *River Rogue*:

> The Coventrys' big sawmills in the suburban village of Pineville had brought other Yankee capital to new Coventry County that bore their name and new people to the newly-established resort hotel at Lancaster, the county site, to bask there, in southern sunshine and the salutary airs of pine forests, to entertain themselves and to look for profitable investments.[183]

Her preoccupation with the wealth and prosperity of this earlier time precipitates Lucy's and Adam's downfall, while revealing the successful future she and the Colonel once anticipated for themselves. It also memorializes a piece of history, the Uplands Hotel at Eastman, which Mark V. Wetherington describes as "the most populous resort" in the Wiregrass region during the late 19th century and "a winter resort for capitalists."[184].

Adam, too, has experienced a decline in his middle age. His younger years are portrayed in language recalling the idealistic, almost superhuman abilities of Ratliff Sutton in *River Rogue*. Adam probably experienced more equality as a raftsman than in his centralized agricultural role since. In her and Adam's conversation regarding his wife, Lucy Hightower comes to realize what Adam once was, before the waning of the timber market and the death of her husband:

> Gazing at her now lean and middle-aged overseer, talking on in his dignified composure, Mrs. Hightower began to see, with some astonishment, the reckless young river rover of twenty years before—the champion axman, raftsman, shot, who accepted the favors of women (their color made them more, not the less, women) along the river bank.[185]

The mention of Adam's sexual persona creates an overt sexual tension between Mrs. Hightower and Adam. She sees him for the first time as a man, an equal, and a potential sexual companion. While this tension is never acted upon nor remarked upon beyond this one passage, it is remarkable that this scene found its way into an agrarian novel, and demonstrates just how far Cheney's views on race had progressed since his earlier novels. Mrs. Hightower's thoughts on Adam

here cause her to recognize her own desire for companion-
ship, and, gazing into her mirror, preparing her hair for a
Methodist missionary meeting, she articulates the main di-
lemma of the novel:

> Almost three weeks had passed since she had
> received Edward Louthan's proposal of mar-
> riage, and she was still torn between the desire
> and reasoning that would take her and her
> children back to Charleston and fear of what
> this might do for her son, Marcellus, and his
> future commitment to the Hightower holding,
> to his father's dream.[186]

Cheney further embellishes the event with sexual and psychological significance when afterwards, walking down the
streets of Riverton, Lucy expresses distaste for nearly every
element of the town, specifically when she observes a sexual
exchange between a brakeman at the railroad tracks and a
black prostitute, who wiggles her hips at him seductively,
which recalls her earlier thoughts about Adam. She also re-
coils at a sexual conversation between men on the porch of
the hotel. She finds further wickedness in a game of marbles
played by her friend Mrs. McLester's sons as an excuse for the
men to hang around an illicit liquor store.

Her later discovery of her son Marse and his friend Jerome Cranford engaged in sexual relations with her heifer resolves her initial uncertainty as to the wisdom of the land sale. Adam, however, comforts her after his later conversation with the boy, in which he becomes assured of Marse's well being. Adam states that the boy "growin' up and he growin' up *all right*." Adam says that Marse is "goin' to be like [the Colonel]"—that "He thinks like the Colonel. And whut he tell you, hits like that—you kin depend on it."[187] In recognizing the merits of the boy, Adam sets up the conclusion to the novel in which Marse's religious conversion and wisdom solely redeem the widow and Adam in light of their respective tragedies.

Similarly, Lucy Hightower, like Micajah Corn, is able to read such future tragedy in the natural environment around her:

> Her surprise bore some realization that events might be making up about her of which she, in her absorption with the ills and contingencies of the moment, was unaware—indeed, that these events might be beginning to transpire. For she perceived the circling gloom. But how could she have anticipated where the Light would lead her?[188]

These last two lines emphasize the fact that despite the portentous, foreshadowing nature of the storm, Lucy, like Micajah is unable to prevent the events of which the storm warns. Troubling events afflict Adam and Lucy in droves. Along with the problems of the Land Deal come Marse's sexual act with the heifer, Adam's letter from his insane wife detailing her suffering in the mental hospital at Milledgeville, and the stroke of Mrs. Hightower's sister.

Adam too recognizes trouble through his senses, although, unlike her, his premonitions are useful to him when he heeds them. When Mrs. Hightower informs him of the status of the land holdings, falsely assuring him that the Wyche field and clay deposits will not be sold, the odor he associates with white people, and inherently, treachery, comes to him: "Suddenly the white smell was at him again, anathema in his nostrils."[189]

Adam's mother also possesses the power to foresee tragedy resulting from the Land Deal. On the night of the hail storm, she warns Adam not to concern himself with freeing his estranged wife Malinda from the mental asylum in Milledgeville: "Son, you needn't worry no mo' 'bout Malinda. She ain't goin' to git well...She comin' here, all right, but 'twon't do us any good—nor harm!"[190] The ambiguity of her next lines serves to increase the tension in the novel as well as foreshadow the later tragedy.

In the guise of warning Adam not to let young Walter Bruce's pet coon into their home, she says: "Hit wuz close, close [...] but hit went on by."[191] When questioned by Adam as to the meaning of her words, she begins to sing a song that eerily echoes the tragic theme of the novel: "Land lines and timber...boat in the River..."[192] The implication of the old woman's words that "it went on by," seems to be that Adam's chance for salvation and economic freedom has passed, that the Land Deal inevitably will go wrong for Adam, and his wife is doomed to remain within the harsh confines of the insane asylum.

Adam and Mrs. Hightower are joined in the novel, not only through their history together or their allegiance to the dead Colonel Hightower, but through the oppressive forces in the town's treatment of them. Upon hearing that Peter Bright has sold the note he held against Adam to the bank, and that the banker Littleton is now demanding payment in full by Adam in order to blackmail him into following their part in the Land Deal, Mrs. Hightower articulates her and Adam's connection:

> I am really amazed at Mr. Littleton—and he is supposed to be my friend and adviser! And Peter Bright, too! It's low down of him!" She started her striding again. "All of them, all of them. Out to do you in, because you are col-

ored and me in, because I'm a woman and a widow."[193]

Adam's plight steadily increases in the novel, his fear of losing the Wyche field becoming extremely probable in light of the widow Hightower's situation and her desire to move the family to Charleston at any cost. The banker Littleton, along with the lawyer Duke, encourage Adam to take their side in confusing Lucy Hightower as to where her real land lines lie. Adam's refusal to cooperate puts him in great peril.

Eventually, the African-American laborer, Kiger Steele, comes to Adam claiming to have knowledge of a letter between Mr. Lincoln, the land buyer, and Oswald Paley, an unscrupulous local profiteer. In the letter, Lincoln announces that the widow has agreed to withdraw the exemption from the Wyche field in exchange for keeping the mineral rights to her land. Kiger's attempt to convince Adam that the widow has forsaken him is in some ways successful. Adam begins to question her faithfulness and rightfully so. Once again, he seeks for the answers in the mythical force of the Wyche field:

> The view grew misty and a current rose up through him, as if from the ground. A current from the old field itself—their experience together—of hunger and fulfillment, of high water and waiting, of sweat and strain and anx-

iousness, but at last the warming sight of a snowstorm of open cotton bolls. Till now. He turned his back on the field and wiped his eyes with his hands.

The Colonel had told him if he brought the field back, he could keep *on* tending it. But the Colonel wasn't here. His word didn't count any more....If he could only *talk* to the Colonel![194]

Adam's realization that he might lose the Wyche field causes him to momentarily falter in his conviction that the power of the field will guide him through the current crisis. Adam's wavering faith in the widow, himself, and the power of the Wyche field, gives birth to a prophetic dream that helps Adam to effect a change in the upcoming events.

In his dream he has returned to the river, rafting timber much like in his younger days. Images of a mythical ghost on old Hannah's Island mingle with memories of the riot in Lancaster and the Lost Mountain Prison in which Adam was unjustly incarcerated after the riot. Hannah was raped and killed by soldiers during the Civil War. Her image merges with that of Mrs. Hightower, implying a metaphorical link between Hannah's fate at the hands of the soldiers and Mrs. Hightower's fate at the hands of the townsmen. Adam is aware of a great lighthouse, and Mrs. Hightower calls to him, urging him to "turn the light on them."[195] Finally, a small raccoon comes to Adam explaining the true location of the lever that operates the light, on the other side of the river. The coon tells him to get in a boat and paddle to the other side of the river, but to "beware of the boat! It belongs to the men on the island."[196] The boat capsizes when Adam attempts to get out of it, but the coon pulls him out of the water. He is able to activate the lever at last, flooding the island with light, allowing Adam to see the "Land-dealers pop, like soap bubbles, as the rays hit them—and Banker Littleton, the biggest of them all, popped like a paper bag."[197] Finally, the coon chastises Adam for trying to "desert us."[198] Adam realizes that the coon is speaking for the whole creation of dumb creatures.

This dream is filled with thematic significance. The coon's statement that Adam "tried to desert us" addresses Adam's abandonment of hope in the Wyche field, the widow, and himself and his secret desire to join the dealers in perpetuating fraud against Mrs. Hightower, thereby securing the field for himself. Through the dream, Adam once again associates the discrimination he felt in the Lancaster race riot, and the loneliness of the Lost Mountain prison with the "Land Dealers" of the town. The power of the river, the mystical power of Hannah's ghost, and the power of the coon all come to Adam's aid in the dream. He realizes that he must shine a great light upon the Land Dealers, exposing their corruption and fraudulence in manipulating the widow into giving up her clay rights and the Wyche field in the sale.

The power of Adam's dream manifests itself in the prevention of his murder by Kiger Steele a few weeks later. Under the guise of a fishing trip, Kiger and Adam set out upon the Oconee to retrieve the Lincoln letter from Oswald Paley and Hinshaw Slappey, who are cutting timber on the other side of the river. Afterwards, they will bring the letter to Mr. Peter Bright who will read it and verify its contents for the illiterate Adam.

Adam, upon starting out on the trip, recognizes Kiger's uneasiness and suspects possible foul play, anticipating Kiger's attempt to shake him out of the boat and drown him. Upon discovering that the name of Kiger's boat is the Green Ghost, Adam remembers Hannah's ghost from his earlier dream, as well as the green color of the boat in the dream. Soon after, Adam recognizes the river cut that he and Kiger are paddling through as the same cut from his previous dream, when he fell out of the boat.

Adam effectively foils this plot by anchoring the boat on a clay root. When Adam is thrown out of the boat, he pulls himself down to the bottom and, using the root for leverage, pulls down on the chain and capsizes Kiger as well. He holds him at bay in the water by alternately pulling or slapping Kiger under, and then swimming away from him just as he has often witnessed a raccoon do to a dog. Afterwards, Adam thanks the coon from his dream for saving his life, and utilizes the situation with Kiger to uncover the corruption of the "Land Dealers."

In a brilliant display of trickery, Adam forces Kiger to hide on the other side of the river, maintaining to the authorities of the county that the man drowned himself because he was "in trouble with some white mens."[199] Adam's plot, while not overtly convincing to Littleton and Paley, nevertheless, puts these men in an awkward situation, especially after Adam produces the torn half of a hundred dollar bill that he found in Kiger's wallet, suggesting that Kiger was employed by Oswald Paley. His mother declares Adam's trick a moral victory for all African-Americans: "But son, you done put a plaster on your ma's ole sore, you done poltice her carbuncle!"[200] Adam's reply reveals his own remaining uncertainty as to the success of his effort for the widow and himself: "I don't know ma. I kept 'em from drownin' me—the low, white trash sons-of-bitches! That's all I know."[201]

Adam regards his victory as slight at best, but his mother, Electra, hardened by her early years in slavery, recognizes Adam's blow to be a redeeming force, one that he achieved at the behest of the mythical power of the river and his own supernatural dream. Electra, emboldened by drink, finally warns Adam of his mistake in taking the young boy Marse along with him, and of trusting the widow Hightower: "'E white, ain't 'e?"[202] In this manner, Adam's mother gives rise to the indeterminacy of Adam's future, being black and agrarian within a society dominated by white men and industry.

Electra's words here prove to be both prophetic and false. The ending of the novel is complicated. She is correct that Adam cannot trust the adult white characters in the novel to see to his interests, but she's wrong about Marse, as his religious conversion ultimately redeems Adam in the novel. Marse's conversion recalls that of Micajah Corn in *Lightwood*. Cheney's treatment of these separate incidents, however, varies greatly, perhaps reflecting Cheney's own conversion to Catholicism under the influence of Allan Tate and Caroline Gordon between the publication of these two novels.

Micajah Corn's conversion in *Lightwood* precipitates a stroke in the man, seals the tragic fate of his son and friends, and affords him no redemption in the novel. Marse's conversion in *This is Adam* is the only redeeming force at the end of the novel, for Adam, Mrs. Hightower, and Marse himself.

The story of Marse's conversion reveals the initial lack of authentic spirituality in Lucy Hightower. She reflects on the disagreeable nature of religion in Riverton: "And it seemed that Riverton had to take its religion, like everything else, raw, sensationally, and fitfully. [...] She wanted [Marse] to experience Christian conversion, certainly—if he hadn't already. But at a revival! That would not be like a Hightower!"[203] Cheney delivers the revival in highly dramatic literary form, culminating in Marse's conversion at the altar and his walking out of the church without acknowledging his mother. Reminiscent of the Darien hurricane in *River Rogue*, a destructive event from nature accompanies the action. Lightning strikes the church, outlining the figure of Marse as he walks slowly away from his mother, and oddly recalling the earlier thunderbolt that hit the barn when Mrs. Hightower discovered Marse and Jerome Cranford engaging in sexual relations with her cow. The fact that these two pivotal events in the novel are accompanied by thunderclaps seems melodramatic and a bit clichéd, but the thunderclaps do serve to reveal a strange connection. In each instance, Mrs. Hightower is embarrassed by and deeply uncomfortable with her son's behavior, but in Christian terms, these events punctuate Marse's sins against God and man and his later forgiveness and repentance for them.

Like Mrs. Hightower, Adam also lacks true religious conviction. Earlier in the novel, overwhelmed by the problems of the land deal, he had found it impossible to pray. Adam's attempted murder follows soon after Marse's conversion and results in the public shaming of Oswald Paley, revealing the apparent relationship of Paley and Kiger Steele to the Northern land buyers and the local land speculators. Adam cautiously refuses to reveal the fact that Kiger and Paley attempted to have him drowned. Martin Slater, the land buyer's lawyer, articulates the new situation to Mrs. Hightower and Adam:

Any letters Paley showed anyone involving us in his scheme were a forgery, let me say![...]There are obviously substantial circumstances to make this letter legal evidence. We will turn it and three others over to you...I think they constitute a basis for prosecuting Oswald Paley for attempted larceny by trick.[204]

The Land Deal goes through, with the exemption of the Wyche field, which the lawyer Slater agrees to lease to Adam for the next ten years for the sum of $100 with the option to renew at the end of that time. The deal is satisfactory for Adam and Mrs. Hightower as well as the Northern buyers.

Later, Marse urges Adam to reveal to Mrs. Hightower the plot to have him drowned: "I tell you, Adam, she's not going to prosecute Paley unless she knows about his trying to have you drowned! She won't prosecute him just for trying to steal her clay."[205] Marse explains that "I would be against prosecuting Paley, too, except for what he did to you, Adam."[206] Adam reminds Marse of Paley's prior betrayal of his father: "Whut that damned copperhead did amounted to *killin'* the Colonel!"[207] Marse replies in the rhetoric of the New Testament that he has "killed" Paley a "thousand times—in my imagination" but that "I don't do it anymore, Adam. I don't. Now I realize it's up to God to settle with Paley."[208] Marse ends the conversation by declaring that Adam is "in slavery" to his hatred of Paley and "I'm free."[209]

Adam does not heed Marse's advice, but the discussion affects Adam in a physical way, causing him to feel the pangs of his own religious conscience: "His hands, holding the boat paddle across his knees, were suddenly cramped by some frantic cross purpose in his muscles and his throat ached."[210] Ultimately, Marse's warning is fulfilled and the Wyche field lost, along with the possibility of prosecuting Paley. Adam, in a stuttering, uneasy speech, explains to the widow Hightower in the final scene of the novel: "Well, this morning, Mr. Kitchum tell me they didn't get no d-deescription of [the land lot] and ain't no lease bin drawn."[211] Adam tells the widow that he knows the whereabouts of Kiger Steele and can provide him as a witness in the trial of Oswald Paley. Mrs. Hightower, obviously affected like Adam by her son's conversion, replies that she is "not spotless, either, in this sorry passage of human affairs."[212] She has returned the evidence against Paley to him and decided to forgive him for his attempted theft. She and Adam exclaim against their respective misfortunes: "Oh, Mrs. Hightower, Mrs. Hightower, Mrs. Hightower! Whut you gone and done! [...] You done ruint me! Ruint me!"Mrs. Hightower replies ambiguously that Adam "ruined me, too! Charleston's gone!"[213]

The emotional anguish of the past months and years envelops Adam and a diverse whirlwind of images flies before him. Within this visual montage, Adam once again associates his unjust arrest at the Lancaster riot and his incarceration in Lost Mountain prison with the faces of Paley, Slappey, and Littleton and the racial adversity he has encountered in Riverton. Images of his wife Malinda locked within the sanitarium mingle with those of his new wife, Babe. This scene culminates with a vision of Marse and his ominous warning: "You're in slavery." Adam lets go of his hatred and pain, and like Marse, embraces Christ.

The final revelations from Adam and Mrs. Hightower proceed in successive paragraphs in a parallel structure referred to by Ashley Brown as "a double post of observation" between Adam and Lucy. Brown maintains quite correctly that the success of the novel is based on this structure: "We move from one to the other, usually in alternating chapters, and the boy Marcellus or Marse is the focus of the drama."[214] Cheney, in his letters to Flannery O'Connor, also emphasizes the significance of this last scene, noting that the ritualistic nature of Adam and Lucy's meetings at the steps outside her home are intended to be "a rhythm of sorts throughout the book, ending with it, I hope for a total significance."[215] The similarities between their final epiphanies are worth noting:

> Her throat constricted and she shut her eyes
> to the rising image of Edward.

There was to be no Indian summer for her. Her title to *wild lands on the banks of the Oconee* had carried an irrevocable commitment! This was Hightower country, father and son, and Marse must grow up in it. Raw, rough, dark land, but somehow it was vital. And not the least of its vitality was in the illiterate mixed negro before her, torn from the womb of sin and slavery and curiously shaped in God's image, the only man alive she had complete confidence in, her son's foster father!"[216]

Mrs. Hightower's rededication to the Wiregrass region and the raising of her son in the shadow of Adam and the likeness of his father is analogous to Adam's final religious resolve.

Adam reflects:

"I know now I'm going to lose the Wyche field. Mr. Kitchin said that Mr. Lincoln didn't want me to have that lease. But I see now what the Colonel saw, lying there in his bed so close to the door. There are more important things! And you don't have to die to find that out but it helps. One of 'em's God's freedom."[217]

God's freedom has erected a new structure in the lives of Adam and the young Marcellus, a character that only truly comes into focus during the latter half of the novel. It is only at the end that Marse displays a wisdom that transcends his youth and immaturity and exerts a redeeming force on the other characters. Cheney utilizes Marse's rhetoric as both the climax of Adam's vision and the crux of his affirmation.

Ultimately, Lucy Hightower's vision of moving to Charleston, along with Adam Atwell's vision of owning and tending the Wyche field are just delusions. The "it" that the Colonel referred to on his deathbed once again comes into play, this time in the wisdom displayed by his son. As in Cheney's earlier novels, *This is Adam* ends tragically with the loss of the family farm in the sale, the loss of Mrs. Hightower's dream of moving to Charleston and marrying her childhood sweetheart, and the loss of the Wyche field and Adam's dream of eventual independence. The seriousness of this blow, however, is cushioned, even negated in the religious affirmation of Adam, Marse, and Lucy at the end of the novel. They decide to hold on to "more important things," the vitality of the wild land of the Oconee flood plain and the relationship of God and man.

From a Christian perspective, the novel ends perfectly, cementing the importance of man's dedication to God. From an African-American perspective, this ending remains problematic. Adam is right back where he started at the beginning of the novel, kneeling at the steps of the Hightower home, submissive to Mrs. Hightower and her son and at the mercy of the "land dealers" in the town, who have every reason to bear him grudges for his help of the white characters. His only redemption comes from adopting the religion of his oppressors. He quite literally submits to the white man's God, the "it" that the Colonel referred to on his death bed. Marse's warning that Adam is "in slavery" to his hatred further complicates this ending, as does the following passage where Adam notes:

> And he realized that there had been behind him all of the time, through the storm, like a mooring mast, the dim shadow of a black-caped and –skirted woman—a blackness that somehow cast a light through his balloon-like transparence, now shriveling and expiring. [218]

Adam here associates the "light" from his dream with the widow Hightower and compares himself with the land dealers of the dream who popped in the light. She and Marse are literally both his ruin and his salvation. It is difficult for a 21st century reader to consider the ending as a triumph for Adam. He may have accepted the white man's religion, but the white man has still failed to accept him.

The strangest question of the novel for me is why Mrs. Hightower feels that Adam has "ruined" her too. How has he caused her to lose her hopes of moving to Charleston? Cheney fails to make this clear. The dreams of Charleston and the affection she feels for Edward are overshadowed by the action and attempted murder of Adam at the end of the novel. Perhaps the answer lies in the earlier, somewhat sexual tension between Mrs. Hightower and Adam and her recognition that Adam was the "only man alive that she had complete confidence in, her son's foster father." Does she then mean that the relationship with Adam has ruined her feelings for Edward and her desire to move to Charleston altogether? If so, then she is ruined, since Riverton society will never allow her to act on her feelings. In fact, Riverton already feels that the relationship between these two individuals is inappropriate. Caroline Gordon calls the relationship between Adam and Mrs. Hightower one in which "they are co-equal because the bond which holds them together is forged by love and mutual understanding."[219] A modern reader may not see them as co-equal exactly, particularly since Adam is still forced to meet Mrs. Hightower at the bottom of the porch steps, but no modern reader can fail to notice the powerful nature of their bond and mutual dependence upon one another.

Notes

[164] Brown, 62.

[165] Cheney, *Lightwood*, 157.

[166] Ibid, 164.

[167] Cheney, *Lightwood*, 223.

[168] Ibid, 224.

[169] Cheney, *The Correspondence of Flannery O'Connor and the Brainard Cheneys*. Letter 48.

[170] Ibid, Letter 68.

[171] Ibid.

[172] Ibid, Letter 73.

[173] Ibid, Letter 74.

[174] Cheney, *This is Adam*, 10.

[175] Ibid, 11.

[176] Ibid, 15.

[177] Ibid, 68.

[178] Ibid, 21.

[179] Ibid, 22.

[180] Ibid.

[181] Ibid.

[182] Ibid, 4.

[183] Ibid, 128.

[184] Wetherington, 88-9.

[185] Ibid, 145.

[186] Ibid, 148-9.

[187] Ibid, 212.

[188] Ibid, 155.

[189] Ibid, 165.

[190] Ibid, 178.

[191] Ibid, 179.

[192] Ibid.

[193] Ibid, 211.

[194] Ibid, 222.

[195] Ibid, 225.

[196] Ibid.

[197] Ibid, 226.

[198] Ibid.

[199] Ibid, 261.

[200] Ibid, 273.

[201] Ibid.

[202] Ibid, 275.

[203] Ibid, 229.

[204] Ibid, 280.

[205] Ibid, 290.

[206] Ibid.

[207] Ibid.

[208] Ibid, 292.

[209] Ibid.

[210] Ibid.

[211] Ibid, 294.

[212] Ibid, 299.

[213] Ibid, 300.

[214] Brown, 62.

[215] Cheney, *The Correspondence of Flannery O'Connor and the Brainard Cheneys*. Letter 48.

[216] Cheney, *This is Adam*, 302.

[217] Ibid.

[218] Ibid, 301.

[219] Gordon, Caroline. "The Novels of Brainard Cheney." *The Lightwood Chronicles*. Stephen Whigham, Ed. Eastman, Georgia: MM John Welda BookHouse, 2012, 45.

6.

Devil's Elbow: Dehumanization and Redemption

As he sat there on the log, still, in the gray lack-light, it came to him. It came over him what this precipitously, perilously, horribly suspended thing was. It was an odor. The sickeningly sweet, ghostly thing, insidiously penetrating smell of rotting human flesh. He had never known it before, but there was no denying it now, for he was saturated with it, from nose to bung. It seeped into the marrow of his bones. His eyes watered of it.

—Brainard Cheney, from his novel *Devil's Elbow*

Devil's Elbow, Cheney's last novel, proves to be his most distinctly modern text and probably the least successful of his novels. Intensely autobiographical, the novel is a sort of sequel to *This is Adam*, chronicling the later years of the character, Marcellus Hightower, from the earlier novel. The mood and tone of the two works, however, vary greatly.

Cheney divides this novel into four parts: *First Return: Judy, Second Return: Melanie, Third Return: Sheila, The Wake: Adam.* This structure reveals the novel's preoccupation with Marcellus's sexual relationships, and the manner in which these mostly failed relationships reflect Marcellus's own struggles with morality and his inability to come to terms with the murder of his childhood friend, David Ransom. Cheney refers to the novel as "the metaphysical unfolding of a murder mystery in which the hero's sense of moral guilt evolves into a redeeming love."[220]

Devil's Elbow departs from Cheney's earlier novels in its distinctly modern style with fragmented chronology. The time line of the novel is difficult to distinguish, and the fragmentary chronology demonstrates the influence of modern literature upon Cheney's writing.

The novel begins with Marcellus's traveling by train from Nashville, where he has been attending Vanderbilt University, back to his hometown of Riverton during the Christmas season of 1926. Marcellus at this time views his immediate present as the aftermath of incredible disaster—the murder of his friend David and the death of his mother—and as a precursor to some inevitable tragedy. Marcellus's perspective proves to be increasingly fatalistic, the obvious result of the trauma of his friend's death and his participation in the intellectual environment of "Nashville's Bohemia."[221]

Marcellus figures his life as futile, leading to inevitable catastrophe and ruin. Sitting in his seat on the train, he hears "a voice in the low wash of time's roar."[222] The "underbeat" of the train's car wheels constitutes a "fell refrain" that, as Marcellus notes, lends to his motion "what he would have called, had it come to it, an eschatological rhythm."[223]

Similarly, Marcellus is able to prefigure his past, as having already led to unspeakable and outrageous violence. At the end of the first chapter, thinking back on his first love, Melanie and his boyhood friend, David Ransom, Marcellus reflects on the innocence of their childhood:

> In the smoker Marcellus took out his pipe to mutter aloud and wag his head. There they all were. On the brink of things. David, Adam, himself. And precocious little Melanie taking them all into her looking glass, into her future—but not seeing—nobody seeing the specter of violence glaring over their shoulders. The roar came closer."[224]

Marcellus's tendency to thus dramatize his life reflects his literary nature as well as his preoccupation with doom and the overwhelming guilt he feels regarding David's death. Although Cheney compels the reader to view Marcellus and his troubles in a serious light, he definitely tends even this early in the novel to suggest pretentiousness in Marcellus's outlook. And the author makes light of the manner in which Marcellus applies his collegiate learning to the understanding of his own life. Marcellus's own admission that the adjective *eschatological* "was a recent acquisition that he sought occasions to use" indicates his eagerness to utilize difficult words to impress others.[225] The effect of this intellectual eagerness, however, is not to satirize students of literature or to paint Marcellus in a comic light. He is a modern figure, endowed with strengths and weaknesses, driven from spirituality by tragedy, and torn between the agrarian lifestyle of Riverton and the Bohemian environment of Nashville.

Marcellus's four returns to Riverton both indicate the necessity of returning to one's roots in order to receive redemption and suggest a preference for the spiritually sound environment of Riverton over the corruption of Nashville society. This preference for the rural and agrarian over the urban and industrial accords thematically with Cheney's earlier works. During each return, Marcellus experiences a sort of epiphany regarding his own life and his sense of responsibility for David's death. As the novel progresses, these epiphanies change from feelings of dejection and futility to those of redemption and love.

During his initial return, Marcellus feels intense guilt over the death of David five years earlier. Marcellus, the novel reveals, sent David into the woods to hunt a group of roosting turkeys, suggesting that the "swamp rat," Buck Fykes, might be able to show him their exact location.[226] After locating Fykes, David entered into a bout of drinking with Buck and two others. An eventual argument resulted in his drowning. Within this context the fell refrain of the car wheels—the eschatological rhythm that Marcellus uses to propel himself back home: "T-Taking you to the turkey roost...t-taking you to the turkey roost"—takes on a wholly new meaning.[227] The turkey roost becomes a metaphor for death, and Marcellus becomes convinced that his own jealousy of David subconsciously prompted him to send the young man to his doom.

Cheney bases this event on the murder of his own childhood friend Robert Willcox, by J. E. Buckhanon and J.C. Thompson in January of 1921. Cheney's fictional account accords in almost exact details with descriptions from the actual trial right down to the details of where Robert's (David's) personal effects were found and Buckhanon's (Fyke's) remarks after the murder about wishing that someone would cut his throat.

The exact events of the murder remain a mystery until the end of the novel, as each of the suspects tells a different story, though all agree that the boy's body was weighted and dumped into the river. Repeated river draggings fail to find any remains, and weeks elapse before the body is found. Marcellus's ultimate trauma from the death occurs when he, an uncle, and a cousin discover David's rotting corpse on an island a few miles above the River Landing. Cheney, in his "I See Sunday" essay, commenting on the novel, notes:

> I drew on autobiographical material for much of *Devil's Elbow*. And, in a categorical way, the fictional murder does parallel history.[...].The circumstance of that murder that dogged me over the years and may be said to have inspired the novel eventually was the finding of my friend's body. That incident in the story is factually presented. But there is a literal sense in which the happening "dogged" me that contributed to my fictional inspiration. I had never before smelled rotting human flesh when I chanced upon the cadaver of my friend, on the upper point of Burnt island (sic), six weeks after his death; "Shorty" Hightower's reaction to this odor, as detailed in the novel, offers an exact description of my actual experience. And it is true that the odor pursued me, pursued me for years.[228]

In the novel, the odor, which Marcellus refers to as "wild bees," plagues him for weeks after finding the body and enduring the autopsy. Years later, when Marcellus finally unravels the mystery of David's death, the odor comes on him again, primarily in sexual situations, and invariably accompanied by impotence.

The immediate aftermath of David's death reveals Marcellus's initial sexual inadequacies. He finds comfort in a family friend, Judy Courtney, whose panties he had gazed upon as a grade school kid. Marcellus reflects that their brief and sad love affair had been a "late-Victorian thing, even to the Freudian undertones."[229] Associating Judy with her chivalrous father and his own Victorian-era mother, Marcellus clings to her after the death of David. One night while walking her home, they engage in a sort of wrestling play, and his hand falls upon her breast. When Judy reveals herself willing, Marcellus briefly fantasizes about ripping her clothes off and having sex with her in the drainage ditch, but then breaks into a run, reflecting that he "was never meant for a caveman."[230] Later they somewhat declare their love for one another and his intentions to "reclaim his grandfather's house for them to live in." He then reflects that "what he really wanted to do [...] was to walk always under the pines, in the moonlight, and hold her hand."[231] Marcellus here reveals that his intentions towards Judy have never been sexual. He holds her up in his mind on a pedestal, as a virginal, Victorian image to be cherished and never ravished, much like his mother.

Judy displays a subliminal awareness of Marcellus's intentions when she begins singing a verse from a song called "Santa Lucia" reminiscent of the Garden of Eden vision Marcellus has of his mother, who is, after all, named Lucy. Marcellus certainly regards her as a saint. Judy ultimately grows bored with the virginal and asexual Marcellus, rejecting him on St. Simon's Island for the more sensual Clyde Dupres. After Marcellus discovers the two of them engaged in some form of intercourse in a hammock outside the home in which they are staying, she goes to the beach with him out of pity and tells him that she is "not noble like you think I am—and like *you* are" and warns him to "forget her."[232]

A futile attempt to prevent the bank from foreclosing on his mother's land holdings prompts Marcellus's initial return to Riverton only six months after her death. At home Marcellus attempts to renew his failed love affair with Judy and attends the delayed trial of Dunk Slitcher (probably based on J. C. Thompson), one of David's murderers. Unfortunately, the loan Marcellus attempts to float on his home place falls through, along with his and Judy's plans for marriage. Then, Dunk Slitcher is released on the testimony of Marcellus's cousin, Grip Jackson. In the face of these events, Marcellus forsakes his family holdings, Judy, and the Wiregrass region and returns to Nashville.

After listening to Marcellus engage in a brief and violent cursing of his surroundings, Adam Atwell, his family's African-American caretaker, notes in his stuttering voice, "I don't know as it does any good to G-Goddamn about it."[233] Marcellus pays no heed to Adam's warning and flees the town of Riverton, headed back into the heart of Bohemia: Nashville.

Cheney's psychological overtones remind one of his earlier novel, *River Rogue*. Just as Ratliff Sutton's preoccupation with his mother's infidelities, his fatherlessness, and his carelessness in the drowning of Poss affects his relationships with women, Marcellus's guilt and sense of responsibility in David's death is irrevocably intertwined with his sexual inadequacies and his "love life." Much of the novel revolves around Marcellus's relationship with Melanie, who later becomes his wife. His jealousy over his incorrect perception that David had made love with Melanie prior to Marcellus, plays a major role in Marcellus's guilt over David's death. These experiences are rife with symbols. Melanie tells him later in college that she had "chewed his sugarcane" when they were younger and she was visiting in Riverton, but Marcellus remembers that David had actually given the young Melanie the piece of sugarcane, just as he had believed at the time that David had deflowered Melanie in the "company" bedroom.

His later experiences with women are fraught with rejection, confusion, and misunderstanding, the theme of abortion constituting a dark and malignant undertone to all of these relationships. At the University of Georgia, he impregnates a girl named Blossom, who nearly dies from an infection derived from several illicit abortion attempts. Marcellus and Blossom subsequently end their relationship. Within Riverton, impregnation, like the river and the crop cycle, implies birth and renewal. At the University of Georgia and within the promiscuous environment of Nashville, pregnancy is fraught with peril, a danger to be avoided at all costs. Marcellus sows destruction and ruin in all of his sexual relationships, both literally and figuratively.

Marcellus's early fears of sexual inadequacy originate in comparison with David, a friend under whose shadow Marcellus has always resided. His own nervousness around girls stands in stark contrast to David's ease with them. Marcellus identifies the common bond between David and him, noting that:

> It wasn't that he had no knowledge of the mystery, the thing that had set him and David apart in the world and drew them together: their fatherlessness. His father had died just a year before David's died. And he had led David into the strange headless state of being a boy without a father, had comforted him before a derisive curiosity on the school grounds: 'Did you cry when your pappy died?'—the cal-

lous jest, the taunt that somehow seemed to slash at your privates. It had bound them together against all boys who had fathers"[234]

The theme of fatherlessness continues from *River Rogue*. Ratliff Sutton also had no father, and he too felt these taunts as sexual, "exposing privates strange and red." David also loses his mother in the novel, which seems to increase their bond even further. Marcellus, however, has sexual insecurities that David does not share. Marcellus, like Ratliff in *River Rogue*, finds himself taunted by accusations of miscegenation, as both Ratliff and Marcellus are to some degree raised by black surrogate fathers. Diggs McMillan accuses Ratliff of being "in the bed" with "niggers", while one of the Slitchers in *Devil's Elbow* notes that Marcellus "lives with niggers—sleeps with 'em, they tell me."[235] While these taunts affect Marcellus sexually, David seems immune to them. Despite their common bond, or perhaps because of it, Marcellus's feelings of inadequacy increase when David loses his virginity prior to Marcellus.

Marcellus, after his return to Nashville, renews his love affair with Melanie, and their subsequent relationship and eventual marriage illustrate the depravity of the Bohemian lifestyle they choose to adopt. In scenes reminiscent of Scott Fitzgerald, Marcellus and Melanie engage in excessive drinking, infidelities, miscarriages, and abortions. Marcellus's frequent vulgarity as well as his decision to be married by the justice of the peace in a cigar store, indicate the couple's total rejection of societal norms and the conventions of spirituality. They hold no respect for the sacrament of marriage. Marcellus frowns at the "bourgeois" nature of their honeymoon, wedding gifts, and the possibility of a church ceremony for their wedding.[236] The couple rejoices at Melanie's loss of her first child and their attempts to avoid impregnation are both frantic and obsessive. Their eventual division seems inevitable as Marcellus increasingly relies on mistresses and prostitutes for his sexual favors. Upon leaving for Riverton to pick up his writing again, Melanie informs him that she is once again pregnant. Marcellus retorts, "You damned well better not do that to me."[237]

Marcellus finishes his first novel to some literary success and is reunited with Melanie in Atlanta. They eventually separate again, and Marcellus returns to Riverton to work on another novel about rafting, obviously, a reference to *River Rogue*, this time eliciting the help of Adam Atwell, a character that stands in stark contrast to Marcellus.

Adam, the African-American overseer of the Hightower plantation, is the hero of Cheney's earlier novel, *This is Adam*. Once again, Cheney utilizes Adam as the representative of the agrarian spirit, a man from an earlier, simpler time. In *Devil's Elbow*, he becomes the voice of reason for Marcellus, a sage of sorts. While working on his rafting novel, Marcellus clearly

feels uncomfortable under Adam's gaze: "[H]is own awareness of how he must have appeared to Adam—still appeared,
clumsily approaching his fortieth birthday—made him feel
more like a dogass than a dogfall."[238]

Marcellus, in an attempt to extract details from Adam regarding timber rafting and the Squatters War, deliberately
endeavors to profit from a lifestyle he has rejected. He neces-
sarily feels guilty under Adam's gaze. On this return, Marcellus ventures to the bedside of his dying cousin, Grip Jackson,
who finally relates to him the true circumstances of David's
death. According to Grip, he, Dunk Slitcher, Buck Fykes, and
David had been drinking at Fykes's place. Grip was aware that
David had been having sex with his girlfriend Agnes and when
drunk, began to feel the grudge more heavily. On the trip back
across the river from Buck's camp, he had knocked David into
the water. When David came up for air, Dunk bashed him on
top of the head with his paddle, and he drowned. Grip super-
vised the weighting of the body, and later told Marcellus's uncle the location when the reward for discovery of the body
climbed to $1000. Marcellus had not found the body by coin-
cidence after all. Marcellus refused the reward money, and his
uncle split the money with Grip. Grip used his share to purchase timber from Marcellus, so the reward money had ironically found its way back into Marcellus's hand.

This revelation serves only to increase Marcellus's guilt,
provoking another attack of the "wild bees," and causing a

long vomiting spell. He seeks solace in the company of Adam and relates the story to him, distraught and searching for the meaning of it all. Here the novel finally reveals the most depth, as Cheney ventures into *theodicean* explanation, exploring why a benevolent God would permit evil. Adam mysteriously reveals God's motivations in David's death, and justifies worldly suffering to Marcellus. Accompanied by the lonesome cries of a whippoorwill, Adam stutters out his wisdom:

> They say the g-good die young. And always, us
> h-helps to do 'em in. Just us ordinary, selfish,
> 'ceitful, arrogant, heedless, sorry sons a bitch-
> es. Sometimes 'e lets a good man be took out
> of the tangle of things. Maybe it looks like 'e
> cuts 'im off. But it ain't so. It ain't never blind.
> Hit for us. H-Hit done to show us up, to show
> our own meanness to us...and our needs.
> Yeah, you guilty, Marcellus...along with Grip.
> And I'm guilty, too.[239]

According to Adam, all of mankind is guilty before God in David's death. The purpose of his dying, ultimately, is to lead the living to a better life.

Marcellus's evolution into redeeming love is not completed here on the banks of the Oconee, although he does come to realize the wicked nature of the lifestyle for which he has forsaken his home. Marcellus reflects that the "gray dirt he was lying on had still been his when he quit it so contemptuously that January day in '26."[240]

Marcellus realizes his life in Nashville has been "an idiot's utopia," a "hooligan's heaven," and that his failure with Melanie originated in his guilt over David's death. These thoughts cause Marcellus to remember his most recent breakup with Melanie and here the novel backtracks in time to cover this previously skipped narrative.

In an attempt to compensate for his previous attitude towards children, Marcellus had discussed the issue of having a child with Melanie only to find the earlier feelings regarding childbirth to be reversed. Marcellus clearly believes that having a child will act as a sort of redemptive act for the couple, but discovers that he has waited too late. In a chilling moment, after Marcellus has threatened to stick pinholes in her diaphragm, she throws his earlier words regarding pregnancy back to him: "You damned well better not do that to me."[241] Her initial resolve soon melts and the two begin a steady stream of unprotected sex without procreation. Eventually the strain wears on their relationship, and Melanie articulates the futility of their predicament to Marcellus. She reveals that his earlier ultimatum for her to get rid of the child before he returned to Nashville precipitated an abortion attempt: "And I did, and bled for seven weeks, ruined myself. And you know it. The vultures have been after me ever since. But now you'll lay it on the operation. Now you're through with me. Well, go, go get you another woman."[242] The two separate. Melanie leaves for Chicago to work on her doctorate, and Marcellus returns to the Wiregrass region to work on his novel.

Marcellus begins to experience impotence accompanied by the smell of David's rotting flesh at every sexual encounter, the first of which is with Agnes, Grip Jackson's widow, who, like Marcellus, shares responsibility in David's death. He can only have successful sex with prostitutes and then only when drunk.

Marcellus soon enlists in the army, and the novel quickly moves from Washington to Dublin and back to Washington, the settings of which are feebly rendered. In Ireland, Marcellus begins a love affair with a beautiful, black-haired woman named Sheila. When Marcellus impetuously asks her to marry him, she finally articulates his failure. Sheila states, "But you're not religious. And you can't be. You don't believe. [...].And nothing to build on, I say—nothing to offer up. Nothing in common, like—like denial, suffering."[243] She clearly sees her Catholicism as well as Marcellus's marital status as barriers to their relationship. Marcellus has not taken his marriage with Melanie seriously enough nor taken responsibility for its failure. He has avoided following Adam's advice, which is to learn from suffering, to become a better person for it. Ultimately, Marcellus has yet to accept God.

The last section of the novel begins with, as Ashley Brown notes, "a final pilgrimage to Adam."[244] Marcellus articulates to Adam the haunting odor of David's corpse, his estranged relationship, and his inability to function sexually. Adam explains that Marcellus and Melanie were "too smart" to have children when they married, then "too late" when Marcellus changed his mind.

Adam reiterates that David did not die for nothing. He explains that David's death has redeemed him: "Hit was a sad but saving smell to me. Has been ever since. Hit's not in your nose, Marcellus, nor neither your head. Hit's in your heart."[245] Marcellus leaves, converted at last by Adam's wisdom. He and Melanie reunite on St. Simon's Island, where he discovers that she has also undergone the process of religious conversion. He reiterates Adam's words to Melanie: "For the murdered hero burdens his followers with the crime—as Adam understood. It's their way to salvation."[246]

Brown notes, "The literary problem of religious conversion remains here," questioning the credibility of the sudden change in Marcellus and Melanie.[247]The idea that the couple convert to Christianity separately, simultaneously, and for different reasons—and that this conversion is responsible both for their reconciliation and redemption seems forced and contrived. This reflects an earnest desire by Cheney to portray his and his wife's own religious conversion in this intensely autobiographical novel.

The relative failure of the novel rests on his attempt to encompass too much ground. The story moves quickly through Athens, Nashville, Washington, and Ireland, covering a period from roughly 1921 through 1945. The transient nature of these settings, along with the weakly developed characters of Hulga, Blossom, and Sheila leave something to be desired. As Brown avers:

> "It is when Cheney returns to his familiar territory along the Ocmulgee and the Altamaha that the novel gains its substance—as in his earlier fiction. One doesn't want to call him simply a regional novelist, but certainly he writes his most powerful scenes out of his knowledge of one segment of his native state. One would say the same thing about most of the best American novelists from Hawthorne on."[248]

The limited success of this novel rests on Cheney's portrayal of the dark undertones of guilt inherent in the Wiregrass region. His portrait of the river and its people, while suggesting the tragedy of being, also affirms life. The river becomes a metaphor for the intransigence of life in the region, but also asserts a natural order to the landscape and the rhythms of subsistence. Adam's character emphasizes the existence of Original Sin, apparent in his and Marcellus's pride and arrogance. Adam both recognizes and laments these qualities. David's death, while tragic and sorrowful, redeems Adam and Marcellus through their suffering. Their fallen nature justifies this suffering, and it is only through Marcellus' recognition of this justification that he is saved.

Notes

[220] Cheney, "I See Sunday," 160.

[221] Cheney, *Devil's Elbow*, 4.

[222] Ibid, 1.

[223] Ibid.

[224] Ibid, 10-11.

[225] Ibid, 1.

[226] Ibid, 29.

[227] Ibid, 1.

[228] Cheney, "I See Sunday," 161.

[229] Cheney, *Devil's Elbow*, 57.

[230] Ibid, 68.

[231] Ibid, 79.

[232] Ibid, 90.

[233] Ibid, 127.

[234] Ibid, 16.

[235] Cheney, *River Rogue, Devil's Elbow*, 23, 37.

[236] Ibid, 146.

237 Ibid, 163.

238 Ibid, 183.

239 Ibid, 195.

240 Ibid, 197.

241 Ibid, 199.

242 Ibid, 209.

243 Ibid, 226.

244 Brown, 67.

245 Cheney, *Devil's Elbow*, 238.

246 Ibid, 251.

247 Brown, 65.

248 Ibid.

7.

Conclusion: Cheney's Tragic Natural Forces

Day came. The surface of the water cleared. It was a milky rust-color and spread about him in thick rumples. Around the tree trunks, it spun in tight whirls. He saw one of his logs hung crosswise between two cottonwoods. Ahead through the trees, he could see the river. It bent out of sight into the distance. He looked behind him in the swamp. There were the ends of other logs along the suck, wabbling up and down. He did not call. Poss was not there.

—Brainard Cheney, from his novel *River Rogue*

Some of the more memorable scenes from *Devil's Elbow*, like those in all of Cheney's novels, involve the Altamaha River and its surroundings. As Cheney himself noted, the river constitutes a "mythopoeic force."[249] It is the source of the spiritual, social, and economic changes experienced by the characters in his novels. The river both kills David and secretly redeems Marcellus Hightower. While dragging the river for David's body, Marcellus reflects:

> It was like looking for your lost memory in another man's mind. Tonight he could hear the muddy Oconee laughing. It was windy cold laughter. That ever-moving, deceptively yielding yellow back, three hundred yards wide and thirty feet deep—yielding nothing.[250]

Marcellus clearly associates the murder with the river, later noting that the absence of David's fraternity pin must suggest "the intransigence and mystery of the river—intransigence and mystery of the murder, too."[251]

On his second return to Riverton, Cheney notes, "Returning to his past was to become a dominant pattern of Marcellus's future. Hero of many faces and one myth, he would come back to the river country three more times in search of them."[252] David's death affects Marcellus in the same way that Poss's drowning in *River Rogue* affects Ratliff Sutton. Indeed, Cheney notes that in both novels, the river contributes "controlling action."[253]

This controlling action serves to warn the characters to respect the forces of nature. Death breeds humility and leads the survivors to salvation. Nature and God rule all in Cheney's writing, and it is significant to note that in *Devil's Elbow*, like *River Rogue*, the main character must return to his home country, away from the city—Nashville and Darien, respectively—to find redemption. In *This is Adam*, like *Devil's Elbow*, redemption comes only through relinquishing personal pride and vengeance to accept God.

Adam, in the final chapter, offers to Marcellus the same advice that Marcellus's mother gave to Adam at the end of *This is Adam*:

> When those white mens hired Kiger to kill me over the swamp deal and I outfoxed 'em and come out on top, I *hated* 'em, shonuff hated 'em—so I still hadn't learned. Your ma finally made me see the light. But some things, it looks like, you never get through learning."[254]

Adam had to give up his hatred to accept God; Marcellus must embrace David's death to achieve salvation. However, the endings of these novels of religious conversion fail to achieve the grandeur of his first two.

Religious conversion occurs in *Lightwood*, but fails to redeem for Micajah Corn. The novel is Cheney's darkest and, perhaps, his most successful. His description of the exploitation of the virgin wilderness is both poignant and gripping. The novel acts as a memoriam to the antebellum period. It does not, however, romantically memorialize the period in the manner of a novel such as *Gone With the Wind*. The characters of *Lightwood* are not wealthy cotton barons. They are hardy woodsmen, perpetuating an existence founded on the rhythms of the natural world, for which they hold a deep, if grudging, respect. *Lightwood* chronicles the inevitable, though lamentable, destruction of a simpler and symbiotic way of life.

Similarly, the novel *River Rogue* dramatically closes without the forced trappings of religious conversion. Ratliff Sutton acquires humility in the face of tragedy. His redemption, though subtle, can only be gained by traveling back to his birthplace on the Oconee River.

The novels occupy a thematic continuum that prizes spirituality and the natural world over technological innovation, materialism, and profiteering. Neither technological nor intellectual progress can offer a ready solution to the innate tragedy of existence, and paradise cannot be made immanent on this earth. For Cheney's characters to survive, they must acquire humility and respect, especially with regard to the river, which looms over his novels, creating a sort of natural order, equivalent to, if not always identical with, the deity. Hatred and revenge offer no satisfaction; rather they precipitate trag-edy.

Thematically sound, Cheney's best writing glows with his descriptions of the landscapes, his rendering of Wiregrass region dialect, and his moving imagery. Certain passages stand out in his work. The reader can hardly forget Ratliff's fight with the alligator in *River Rogue,* clearly in the frontier tradition of tall tales. The raftsman Bud True, as a joke on young Ratliff, plunges a corner of their raft into a nest of alligators asleep on the bank. One of the larger creatures leaps onto the raft. In desperation, Ratliff jumps onto the alligator's back and both splash into the water in a frenzied wrestling match. Bud True's later recounting of the event in the Darien tavern resounds with poetry:

> Yeah, I know. Y'all kill stray house cats, usin' a shotgun—buckshot—a-pullin' both barrels. [...]. I stood theah and seen this half-a-peck of gall 'n' gizzard throw a twelve-foot 'gaitor. I mean crawl on top of 'im and stay theah [...].But after 'bout half 'n hour, heah 'e come swimmin' back with one hand. [...].I thought the gaitor had got the other un, but, hell naw, he 'uz a-holdin' the 'gaitor's eyeballs in it. [255]

Here Cheney skillfully renders the dialect of the region without artifice, portraying the natural alliteration and rhythm of the speech. The story of the alligator fight, while mythical, and somewhat reminiscent of the tall tales of Old Southwest humor, is based on a factual incident involving Cheney's uncle, Drew Cheney.

Other brilliantly portrayed incidents in that novel occur when Ratliff runs a low floating raft made of sweetgum timber underneath another raft booming the river and pops out the other side unscathed, or when he refuses to sell his timber in Darien and decides to float his raft back upstream on the rising tide of the mouth of the Altamaha. Here the reader can envision the raft depart from the dock in an ever-widening arc, and then begin to float upstream against the current in a scene both realistic and magical. Cheney portrays the subtle nuances of life in this neglected region and applies them in epic fashion to the human condition.

The similarity in the endings of the last two novels begs for notice. Cheney ends *This is Adam* somewhat ambiguously. Although Adam has triumphantly outsmarted the local profiteers, he wallows in anguish with the realization that these villains will go unpunished. Lucy Hightower explains that he must surrender his hatred to reach salvation—that the punishment of these men will have to be left up to God. Adam must let go of his pride and arrogance, just as Marcellus must end his mourning over David Ransom in *Devil's Elbow*. Both characters forsake their personal prejudices and anguish for a deeper, more spiritual salvation.

Cheney writes of his own work:

> Scattered over thirty years, in four novels, I have sought to celebrate the story of the Altamaha and its people. This I have done with some sense of my role as a historian. But a recent return to the Altamaha and a rereading of these forgotten novels has brought to me their prophesy [sic], in the revelation of the river as a deliverer, now delivered.[256]

In his 1976 essay, " '*Look a, look a yonder, I see Sunday, I see Sunday*', " discussed previously, Cheney delights in the literal aspects of the river's redemption. Concerned with the plans by the Altamaha Basin Commission to change the Altamaha river system into a barge channel, Cheney celebrates the destruction of these plans, based on the redeeming factor of the river—that its very intransigence and unpredictability acts as a natural sewage treatment plant for the millions of settlers of the region. He refers to the river as "the hidden Providence of the health of a million and a quarter of my fellow Georgians."[257] Cheney notes that the characters of his novels would have not only spurned such an action by the

Basin Commission, but would have found the attempt both comic and futile.

The river for Cheney and for his characters cannot be bound or changed by humans. It is a permanent, but dynamic, part of the natural world, endowed with cyclical properties of rebirth. Man cannot control nature, and Cheney brings Snake Sutton back to life in his essay to scoff at the efforts of the engineers, noting that the river would defy any dams and pop up, "another reptile in another swamp." That is the lesson learned not only by Ratliff Sutton, but by Marcellus Hightower and Adam Atwell, as well.

Micajah Corn never learned it, and his ignorance precipitates his lack of redemption at the end of *Lightwood*. Micajah's frustration over his inability to effect change in his environment, to exact his own sort of justice on the profiteers and the agents of the timber company, results in his forsaking every principle his family and his lifestyle ever stood for. He sells out his friends and family, but more importantly, he sells out himself and his own way of life.

Micajah was rightly frustrated and outraged with Calhoun Calebb's sexual violation of his daughter and the corrupt manner in which Calebb had enlisted Micajah's son Littleton into his schemes of assassination against the company. He felt that his own code had been violated, and he recognized his own guilt in these events. He had brought up his son to value punishing the company over tending the fields, and that was his first and chief mistake. His outrage and his hatred of Calebb caused a stroke in the old man, one that should have humbled him and resigned him to return to the tending of his fields. Yet his own sense of self-righteousness, coupled with his atavistic desire to see the "wrongdoers" punished, preempts a most dishonorable act—the testifying against his own friends and family. It was a disgraceful deed, both in Cheney's novel and in history. And while the historical Lem Burch's name has resounded in infamy throughout the Wiregrass region for the last hundred years, Cheney's Micajah Corn returns to his home only to find his lands stolen by the very company whose right to plunder he had inadvertently defended with his testimony.

Ultimately, *Lightwood* stands as the most memorable of Cheney's novels, if only because of the brutal reality that Micajah faces after the trial, and the harsh moral lesson that it teaches. Ratliff, Marcellus, and Adam learned the hard way, but Micajah never learned at all.

Taken together, Cheney's Altamaha novels paint a vivid portrait of a historically neglected region and time period. As he notes, he has written his novels "with some sense of [his] role as a historian."[258] Cheney grew up in the post-Reconstruction era, and witnessed firsthand the destruction of an earlier culture that, while grotesque and brutal in many ways, possessed an ideal that Cheney still found relevant during the waning days of his life. Born at the beginning of the

20th century and dying at the end of it, Cheney watched as the history he sought to preserve in his writing subsided under the endless grind of industrialization and progress. The waning of the timber and rafting industries, coupled with the suffering and deprivation that occurred during the Great Depression, painted a bleak portrait of life in the South. Immersed in Agrarianism at Vanderbilt, Cheney utilized this new school of writing to make sense of the past and present of the Wiregrass region. This lens enabled Cheney to identify the sacred relics of the region and to demonstrate their importance and redemptive power for human beings. Among these were the Altamaha River and its tributaries, the land, the crops, and family. Cheney's novels faithfully weave together history and fiction to preserve in text a forgotten culture. Their importance as history and as literature must not be underestimated.

Notes

249 Cheney, "I See Sunday," 160.

250 Cheney, *Devil's Elbow*, 59.

251 Ibid, 63.

252 Ibid, 112.

253 Cheney, "I See Sunday," 160.

254 Cheney, *Devil's Elbow*, 235.

255 Cheney, *River Rogue*, 64-5.

[256] Cheney, "I See Sunday," 160.

[257] Ibid, 167.

[258] Ibid, 156.

Acknowledgements

Jane Walker and Chris Trowell helped me with research back in 2003 when I was initially writing the bulk of this work at Valdosta State University as a master's thesis. Their publication, *The Dodge Land Wars* (2004) was also an asset.

Dr. John Hiers at VSU greatly encouraged me as a young grad student. He chaired my thesis committee and brought Drs. Byron Brown and Jim Hill on board. All three were excellent editors, whose language made its way into this work.

Addie Briggs's book, *They Don't Make People Like They Used To,* was one of my favorite reads as a boy. Mrs. Briggs's book inspired my interest in these events historically.

Stephen Whigham at MM John Welda BookHouse has been gracious enough to edit and publish these pages, along with the novels of Brainard Cheney. All fans of Mr. Cheney's work owe Mr. Whigham a huge debt but none as great as mine.

My grandparents, Woody and Barclay Williams, first introduced me to the novels of Brainard Cheney. I learned a lot over the years perusing their bookshelves.

My parents, Mike and Felicia Williams, taught me a love of literature. My mother literally taught me to read before I entered school and honed my skills later when she was my first grade teacher.

My wife Jana and my daughters, Joley and Sarah Kate, are my inspiration for everything.

References

Works by Brainard Cheney

Cheney, Brainard. *Lightwood*. Eastman, Georgia: MM John Welda BookHouse, 2012, (1939).

—. *River Rogue*. Eastman, Georgia: MM John Welda BookHouse, 2013, (1942).

—. *This is Adam*. Eastman, Georgia: MM John Welda BookHouse, 2012, (1958).

—. *Devil's Elbow*. Eastman, Georgia: MM John Welda BookHouse, 2012, (1969).

—. Foreword. *Lightwood*. By Brainard Cheney. Washington, DC: Burr Oak Publishers, 1984.

—. Letter to Emily Narin. 13 May 1983. From the Library of Norwood Davidson, McRae, Georgia.

—. "Look-a, Look-a Yonder—I See Sunday, I See Sunday! Or, a Deliverer, Delivered." *The Southern Review* 12 (1976): 156-167.

—. Letter To Flannery O'Connor. 13 January, 1957. Letter 48 of *The Correspondence of Flannery O' Connor and the Brainard Cheneys.*

—. Letter to Flannery O'Connor. 8 September, 1961. Letter 138 of *The Correspondence of Flannery O'Connor and the Brainard Cheneys.* 140.

Additional Works

Beauchamp, Wilton and David Matchen. "The Cheney-O'Connor Letters." *Publications of the Missouri Philological Association 9* (1984): 78-85.

Briggs, Addie Garrison. *They Don't Make People Like They Used To*. McRae, Georgia: Elspeth Enterprises, 1985.

Brown, Ashley. "The Novels of Brainard Cheney." *The Chattahoochee Review*. Spring (1998): 56-65.

Davidson, Donald. *The Tennessee*. Volume One. Nashville: J. S. Sanders and Company, 1946.

Erwin, Marion. *The Land Pirates*. Savannah: The Morning News Print, 1891.

Malvasi, Mark G. *The Unregenerate South: The Agrarian Thought of John Crowe Ransom, Allen Tate, and Donald Davidson*. Baton Rouge: LSU UP, 1997.

Muster Roll of Company B, 49th Regiment. *Research Online.net*. Web. 27 September 2013. Also: "49th Regiment, Georgia Infantry." Confederate Georgia Troops. National Park Service. 18 September 2013. Web. 27 September 2013.

Presley, Delma. Introduction. *Lightwood*. By Brainard Cheney. Washington D. C.: Burr Oak Publishers, 1984.

Rubin, Louis D. Introduction. *I'll Take My Stand: The South and the Agrarian Tradition*. New York, NY: Harper Torchbook, 1962.

Stephens, C. Ralph, Ed. Introduction. *The Correspondence of Flannery O'Connor and the Brainard Cheneys*. Jackson: University Press of Mississippi, 1986. .

Sullivan, Buddy. *Early Days on the Georgia Tidewater: the Story of McIntosh County and Sapelo*. Darien, Georgia: Darien News, 1990.

Talley, J. N. *The Dodge Lands and Litigation: A Report Delivered Before the Georgia Bar Association, June 4, 1925.* Tybee Island, Georgia: Georgia Bar Association, June 4, 1925.

Walker, Jane and Chris Trowell. *The Dodge Land Troubles: 1868-1923.* Fernandina Beach, Florida: Wolfe Publishing, 2004.

Warren, Robert Penn. "Introduction." *River Rogue.* Washington, DC: Burr Oak Publishers, 1982. 1-3.

Warren, Robert Penn. *Talking With Robert Penn Warren.* Eds. Floyd C. Watkins, John T. Hiers, Mary Louise Weaks. Athens: University of Georgia Press, 1990.

Wetherington, Mark. *The New South Comes to Wiregrass Georgia: 1860-1910.* Knoxville: University of Tennessee Press, 1994.

Young, Thomas Daniel. Introduction. *The Tennessee.* Volume One. Nashville: J. S. Sanders and Company, 1991.

INDEX

THE LIGHTWOOD HISTORY COLLECTION

Book 1: *The Lightwood Chronicles: Murder and Greed in the Piney Woods of South Georgia, 1869-1923, being the true story of Brainard Cheney's novel, Lightwood* compiled by Stephen Whigham

Book 2: *Lightwood* by Brainard Cheney

Book 3: *River Rogue* by Brainard Cheney

Book 4: *This is Adam* by Brainard Cheney

Book 5: *Devil's Elbow* by Brainard Cheney

Book 6: *They Don't Make People Like They Used To* by Addie Garrison Briggs

Book 7: *Rivers, Rogues, and Timbermen in the Novels of Brainard Cheney* by Michael Williams, Jr.

Book 8: *When Theo Met Meta: A History of the Coleman-Shaw Families of Valdosta, Georgia* by Daniel Shaw Coleman

www.ingramcontent.com/pod-product-compliance
Lightning Source LLC
Chambersburg PA
CBHW020453100426
42813CB00031B/3348/J